PRAISE FOR YOHURU RASHIED WILLIAMS AND *TEACHING U.S. HISTORY BEYOND THE TEXTBOOK: SIX INVESTIGATIVE STRATEGIES, GRADES 5-12*

"No longer is history something to be ingested and regurgitated on a test, but rather something that absorbs the intellectual imagination of the learner. That is a rare quality in good teaching. The author has done a marvelous job of bridging what are otherwise conflicting paradigms."

—Lynn E. Nielsen
Professor of Education, University of Northern Iowa

"This book offers experienced social studies teachers endless ideas and inspiration to revitalize their classrooms so that students look forward to learning social studies, especially learning experiences placed in their own communities."

—Nancy P. Gallavan
Professor, University of Central Arkansas

"An excellent guide for making history a compelling subject to students through the use of sleuthing and crime analysis metaphors and techniques. Any teacher using the models outlined in the book will find his or her classes more exciting for all involved."

—Eugene F. Provenzo, Jr.
Professor, University of Miami

"Williams presents engaging and unique strategies from his broad range of experience. The connections between historical events and the polemics and mysteries of crime scenes make history learning a thrill."

—Brett Piersma
Social Studies Teacher, Santa Ynez Valley Union High School District, California

"This is not your typical social studies methods book by any means. Williams' highly readable prose shows a deep respect for the marriage of American history content and teaching."

—Elaine Wrisley Reed
Retired Executive Director, National Council for History Education

"Williams' passion for helping teachers look at content in new ways and with clever devices to engage their students is precisely what we need. This informative and well-designed book challenges educators to think outside of the box."

—Dennis Denenberg
Professor Emeritus, Millersville University

"Great teachers are national treasures, and Yohuru Williams is one of them. In this book he shares ideas and teaching methods. He also includes some terrific historic vignettes."

—Joy Hakim
Author

"Dr. Williams is one of the most knowledgeable and exciting History Education presenters in the nation. Finally, teachers will have the opportunity to read, digest, and then implement these fantastic teaching methods into their lessons.

—Kevin T. Brady
President, American Institute for History Education

Teaching U.S. HISTORY Beyond the Textbook

Six Investigative Strategies, Grades 5–12

Yohuru Rashied Williams
Foreword by James Percoco

A Joint Publication

For information:

Corwin Press
A SAGE Company
2455 Teller Road
Thousand Oaks, California 91320
www.corwinpress.com

SAGE Ltd.
1 Oliver's Yard
55 City Road
London EC1Y 1SP
United Kingdom

SAGE India Pvt. Ltd.
B 1/I 1 Mohan Cooperative
   Industrial Area
Mathura Road, New Delhi 110 044
India

SAGE Asia-Pacific Pte. Ltd.
33 Pekin Street #02-01
Far East Square
Singapore 048763

Printed in the United States of America

Library of Congress Cataloging-in-Publication Data

Williams, Yohuru R.
   Teaching U.S. history beyond the textbook : six investigative strategies, grades 5–12/Yohuru Rashied Williams.
      p. cm.
"A joint publication with the American Institute for History Education."
Includes bibliographical references and index.
ISBN 978-1-4129-6620-7 (cloth)
ISBN 978-1-4129-6621-4 (pbk.)
   1. United States—History—Study and teaching.   2.   Teaching—Methodology.
3. Teaching—Philosophy. 4. Education—Study and teaching—United States. I. Title.

E175.8.W555 2009
973.071—dc22   2008026480

This book is printed on acid-free paper.

08   09   10   11   12   10 9 8 7 6 5 4 3 2 1

Acquisitions Editor:	Carol Chambers Collins
Editorial Assistant:	Brett Ory
Production Editor:	Amy Schroller
Copy Editor:	Monica Burden
Typesetter:	C & M Digitals (P) Ltd.
Proofreader:	Kevin Gleason
Indexer:	Sheila Bodell
Cover Designer:	Scott Van Atta

Contents

Foreword

It is a little known fact among the general public that Abraham Lincoln was fascinated with inventions. In 1849 Lincoln applied for a patent, having created a device designed to lift river flat boats over shoals. Patent Number 6469 is the only patent on file submitted by an American president. The sixteenth president also understood the power of education. In an 1859 speech before the Wisconsin State Agricultural Society, Lincoln argued that "every head should be cultivated." In the same speech Lincoln claimed that humanity's greatest invention was the creation of words, because he believed words provided a way one could communicate with "the dead, the absent, and the unborn."

Readers of Yohuru Rashied Williams' incisive new contribution to the field of history education literature will be very pleased with the book they are holding in their hands. How fitting that Williams, in the year we celebrate the bicentennial of the birth of America's greatest president, would tap into this element of the Lincoln legacy. How fitting, too, that Williams is an educational inventor of sorts, as well. Mr. Lincoln would be pleased.

Creative in every aspect of the word, *Teaching U.S. History Beyond the Textbook: Six Investigative Strategies, Grades 5–12* will help history teachers to move well beyond the constraining boundaries of traditional history textbooks, empowering teachers to think and teach outside of the box, while at the same time empowering their students to think more critically, historically, and creatively. The strategies developed by Williams, a one-time classroom teacher, are very relevant today even in the face of the standards-based movement. Here teachers can learn how the lesser known figures of American history can be brought to life, in a lively fashion, that integrates best practices while at the same time addressing larger themes of America's past. Take the case of Ota Benga, an African pygmy brought to the United States at the turn of the last century and put on display in the Monkey House of the Bronx Zoo as the "missing link," by well intentioned folks, in the name of science and knowledge. On the surface the story of Benga may seem trivial, an anachronistic tale of a New York local curiosity. But digging further and placing this story within a larger historical context and framework, we see under William's deft hand how much the

Benga tragedy reflects a larger national phenomenon, the large reach of scientific racism into an America of Jim Crow, blackface, and *Plessey v. Ferguson*. Remember, the Bronx Zoo is not in Birmingham, Alabama.

Through the creative use of stories like that of Ota Benga, Williams provides teachers a window into how to get their students to look deeper into a story. Using strategies skillfully modeled on themes from today's popular culture, teachers can guide their students into actual hands-on history. By becoming interpreters of evidence left by the past, students become detectives doing the rigorous digging so necessary to the study and practice of history. Honoring the diversity of voices from our past as well as recognizing the voices of today's secondary-level history teachers, readers will be inspired, and are indeed encouraged, to find their own particular, singular ways to enliven their history curriculum and are encouraged to take the necessary risks so critical to authentic learning and teaching.

Teaching U.S. History Beyond the Textbook offers a dynamic approach and gives teachers many options from which to choose. Lively teacher-friendly prose is invigorated by real-world experiences that Williams brings to his narrative. This is not pedagogical theory being offered, but the real-world "stuff" of education that makes learning active and organic. The classroom environment as envisioned here by Williams truly becomes a history laboratory.

Pedagogically sound, inspired, relevant, and rich, Yohuru Williams' contributions in this book demonstrate what people have known all along about good teaching and what makes a difference in the lives of students we encounter. Even Honest Abe knew this, reminding people in Springfield, Illinois, in 1852 that "history is philosophy teaching by example." *Teaching U.S. History Beyond the Textbook* embodies this timeless hallmark.

Williams has provided for you the formulae. Now it is your turn to set the example.

—James Percoco
Author and historian

Acknowledgments

This book would never have been possible without the assistance of many supportive friends and colleagues.

I am most grateful to my good friend Dr. William "Bill" Ross for encouraging me to write this book. I am similarly indebted to Dr. Kevin Brady, president of the American Institute for History Education, and Mrs. Elaine W. Read, the former executive director of the National Council for History Education, for their support and encouragement in this regard.

I wish to acknowledge the generosity of my colleagues at Fairfield University in taking time to review and help me with the manuscript. I am particularly grateful to Dr. Elizabeth Hohl and Dr. William Abbot for their insightful and creative comments, and more generally for their incredible friendship. Mr. James Percoco of West Springfield High School (VA) and Mr. Kevin Staton of Fairfield High School (CT) also reviewed parts of the manuscript and made helpful comments. Their friendship and professional collaboration meant a great deal to me. Dr. Steven Newton of Delaware State University and Dr. Tamara Brown of Bowie State University also contributed critical insight at various stages during the development of the manuscript: my deepest thanks to them as well.

Over the years a number of teachers, colleagues, and education specialists have shared their insights on the methods presented in this book. In this respect, I am especially thankful to Mrs. Laura Wakefield of the Florida Virtual School, Dr. Dennis Denenberg, professor emeritus at Millersville University, Dr. Kimberly Gilmore, historian for the History Channel, and Dr. Thomas Connors at the University of Northern Iowa. I am likewise indebted to an amazing group of master teachers for all of their input and inspiration. They are Mr. Melvin Garrison, Philadelphia Office of Curriculum and Instruction (PA); Mrs. Beth Scarborough, Austin Elementary School (GA); Mrs. Lucinda Evans, French Middle School (KS); Mr. James McNeil, Silver Bluff High School (SC); Mr. David Byrd, Elk Grove Unified School District (CA); Mrs. Chris Sink, Hockinson Middle School (WA); Mr. Fred Freitas, Gates Intermediate School (MA); Mr. John Dube, Timberlane Regional High School (NH); Mrs. Fran Macko, Middle School Instructional Specialist (NY); Mrs.

Lannie Leber, Project Director of Content and Continuity (NY); Dr. Theresa Jacobs and Mr. Al Jacobs, Wiregrass History Consortium (GA); Mr. Mike Bruner, Chanute High School (KS); and Dr. Benjamin Ridgeway retired Office of Curriculum Instruction (GA). The anonymous reviewers of the original book proposal and subsequent first draft made invaluable recommendations for improving the manuscript. I hope their suggestions are adequately reflected in this final version and that they will be satisfied with the outcome.

I am grateful to Fairfield University and the American Institute for History Education for funding that assisted in the completion of this manuscript. Special thanks to Brett Ory at Corwin Press for fielding my numerous inquiries and requests. Also very special thanks go to Susan Liddicoat for her masterful editing of the final manuscript. Last but certainly not least, my deepest thanks and appreciation go to Carol Collins, my editor at Corwin Press, for her energy and enthusiasm throughout the production of this book. Every author should have the good fortune to work with such an editor.

I gratefully acknowledge Mr. Kevin Tuma, *Harper's Weekly*, and the University of Utah for allowing me to reproduce copyrighted material.

I also would like to thank my family, my wife Karlyn, and especially my three favorite junior detectives, my children Mason, Asa, and Ella for their love and patience while I was busy writing this book. They are truly a blessing.

My apologies if I have inadvertently failed to acknowledge anyone to whom thanks is due. In spite of the many eyes that have pored over these pages there will of course be errors, omissions, and over-simplifications. I take sole responsibility for these, while hoping that the rest of the book makes up for any deficiencies by inspiring new insights and methods of creativity into teaching American History.

—Yohuru Rashied Williams, 2008

Publisher's Acknowledgments

Corwin Press would also like to thank the following reviewers:

Kevin T. Brady
President
American Institute for History Education, LLC
Swedesboro, NJ

Shari Hills Conditt
Social Studies Instructor
Woodland High School
Woodland, Washington

Thomas Connors
Associate Professor
University of Northern Iowa
Cedar Falls, Iowa

Dennis Denenberg
Professor Emeritus
Millersville University

Nancy P. Gallavan
Professor
University of Central Arkansas
Conway, Arkansas

Stephanie Van Hover
Associate Professor, Social Studies Education
University of Virginia
Charlottesville, VA

Lynn E. Nielsen
Professor of Education
University of Northern Iowa
Cedar Falls, Iowa

Marc Pierlott
Humanities Teacher
Carusi Middle School
Cherry Hill, NJ

Brett Piersma
Social Studies Teacher
Santa Ynez Valley Union High School District
Santa Ynez, California

Eugene Provenzo
Professor
School of Education, University of Miami
Coral Gables, Florida

Elaine Wrisley Reed
Executive Director (Retired)
National Council for History Education
Westlake, OH

About the Author

Yohuru Rashied Williams is associate professor of history at Fairfield University and the vice president for history education for the American Institute for History Education. He is the author of *Black Politics/ White Power: Civil Rights Black Power and Black Panthers in New Haven* (2000) and editor of *A Constant Struggle: African-American History From 1865 to the Present, Documents and Essays* (2002). He is the co-editor of *In Search of the Black Panther* (2006) and *Liberated Territory: Toward a Local History of the Black Panther Party* (2008).

Introduction

History Education—
A Matter of Life or Death?

> The notion that students must first be given facts and then at some distant time in the future will "think" about them is both a cover-up and a perversion of pedagogy. . . . One does not collect facts he does not need, hang on to them, and then stumble across the propitious moment to use them. One is first perplexed by a problem and then he makes use of the facts to achieve a solution.
>
> —Professor Charles G. Sellers,
> paraphrased by S. Samuel Shemis, May 1969

Mississippi Representative Roger F. Wicker (CNN, 2003), during a visit to his home district in 2002, asked a group of advanced-placement high school history students to identify the unalienable rights so eloquently enumerated by Thomas Jefferson in the Declaration of Independence. He was greeted with empty stares. Undaunted, the Republican congressional representative sought to assist the students. "Among these are life," Wicker cheerfully provided, "and. . . ." "Death?" offered one brave student, puncturing the silence. Wicker was stunned. "It's not so much that they don't know the rote phrases and facts," he explained later. "It just demonstrates a real gap in the education of young Americans." Far from an anomaly, Wicker's encounter with these students quickly came to symbolize everything that seemed to be wrong with history and social studies education in the United States.

1

Wicker's experience came in spite of significant work on improving historical literacy among young people, most notably through the work of the Bradley Commission, the National Council for History Education (NCHE), the American Institute for History Education (AIHE), and the Teaching American History (TAH) Grants programs. The yeoman work of these organizations, and others, has produced real results if not as swiftly as some would have hoped. In 2001, for instance, the federally financed National Assessment of Educational Progress (NAEP) found that merely 43% of schoolchildren evidenced a basic knowledge of United States history. In 2007, a similar study by NAEP showed a modest but respectable increase in basic historical knowledge among twelfth graders to 47%. Despite this progress, there is some concern that the numbers game may undermine support for the TAH program since the report's release coincided with discussions about continuing support for "No Child Left Behind," the Congressional act, whose primary emphasis on mathematics and reading has shouldered much of the responsibility for fiscal retrenchment in other subjects, including history and social studies. (For a useful and accessible discussion of history education reform and the problems inherent in testing and history and social studies education, see Wineburg, 2004.)

It is not my intent here to summarize this debate or revisit its many dimensions, but simply to acknowledge how in this environment, questions about how to improve historical literacy have been center stage among history and social studies professionals. The Bradley Commission (1989) led the way in identifying 13 habits of mind students have to practice to learn history effectively:

Habits of Mind

1. Understand the significance of the past to their own lives, both private and public, and to their society.

2. Distinguish between the important and the inconsequential, to develop the "discriminating memory" needed for a discerning judgment in public and personal life.

3. Perceive past events and issues as they were experienced by people at the time, to develop historical empathy as opposed to present-mindedness.

4. Acquire at one and the same time a comprehension of diverse cultures and of shared humanity.

5. Understand how things happen and how things change, how human intentions matter, but also how their consequences are shaped by the means of carrying them out, in a tangle of purpose and process.

6. Comprehend the interplay of change and continuity, and avoid assuming that either is somehow more natural, or more to be expected, than the other.

7. Prepare to live with uncertainties and exasperating, even perilous, unfinished business, realizing that not all problems have solutions.

8. Grasp the complexity of historical causation, respect particularity, and avoid excessively abstract generalizations.

9. Appreciate the often tentative nature of judgments about the past, and thereby avoid the temptation to seize upon particular "lessons" or history as cures for present ills.

10. Recognize the importance of individuals who have made a difference in history, and the significance of personal character for both good and ill.

11. Appreciate the force of the nonrational, the irrational, the accidental, in history and human affairs.

12. Understand the relationship between geography and history as a matrix of time and place, and as context for events.

13. Read widely and critically in order to recognize the difference between fact and conjecture, between evidence and assertion, and thereby to frame useful questions.

Source: From the Bradley Commission on History in Schools. *Building a History Curriculum: Guidelines for Teaching History in Schools.* Westlake, OH: National Council for History Education, 1995, p. 9.

These intellectual skills are needed if students are to tackle successfully the complexity of historical analysis. But what is the benefit of their developing these habits of mind? As NCHE (2007) explains, "Historical analysis develops mental perspectives and modes of thoughtful judgment that students can apply to their lives in addition to their formal study of history."

But how do we as history teachers get students to make the kind of mental commitment necessary to engage in historical analysis? Many outstanding teachers, educational specialists, and scholars, including James Percoco, Fred Drake, Lynn Nelson, Peter Stearns, Sam Wineburg, Dennis Dennenberg, and Joy Hakim, have done important and substantive work in this area either through their research or by conceptualizing new ways to think about and teach history.

Teaching History

Summarizing the vast body of literature on history and social studies education is not the focus of this book. There are, however, numerous works to which I am partial for their influence on my own teaching. These include

Calder, L. (2006). Uncoverage: Toward signature pedagogy for the history survey. *Journal of American History, 92,* 1358–1370.

Davidson, J. W. & Lytle, M. H. (1982). *After the fact: The art of historical detection.* New York: Knopf.

(Continued)

(Continued)

Denenberg, D. & Roscoe, L. (2001). *50 American heroes every kid should meet.* Brookfield, CT: Millbrook Press.

Drake, F. & Nelson, L. (2005). *Engagement in teaching history: Theory and practices for middle and secondary teachers.* Upper Saddle River, NJ: Pearson/Merrill/Prentice Hall.

Fitzgerald, F. (1979). *America revised: History schoolbooks in the twentieth century.* New York: Vintage Books.

Hakim, J. (2002). *A history of US.* New York: Oxford University Press.

Kohn, A. (1999). *The schools our children deserve: Moving beyond traditional classrooms and "tougher standards."* Boston: Houghton Mifflin Company.

Loewen, J. (1996). *Lies my teacher told me: Everything your American history textbook got wrong.* New York: Simon & Schuster.

Percoco, J. A. (1998). *A passion for the past: Creative teaching of U.S. history.* Portsmouth, NH: Heinemann.

Percoco, J. A. (2001). *Divided we stand: Teaching about conflict in U.S. history.* Portsmouth, NH: Heinemann.

Sizer, T. (1992). *Horace's school: Redesigning the American high school.* Boston: Houghton Mifflin Company.

Spoehr, K. T. & Spoehr, L. W. (1994). Learning to think historically. *Educational Psychologist, 29,* 71–77.

Stearns, P., Seixas, P. & Wineburg, S. (2000). *Knowing, teaching & learning history: National and international perspectives.* New York: New York University Press.

Trifan, D. D. (1997). Active learning: A critical examination. *Perspectives, 35*(3), 23–28.

Wiggins, G. & McTighe, J. (1998). *Understanding by design.* Alexandria, VA: Association for Supervision and Curriculum Development.

Wineburg, S. (2001). *Historical thinking and other unnatural acts: Charting the future of teaching the past.* Philadelphia: Temple University Press.

Yarema, A. E. (2002). A decade of debate: Improving content and interest in history education. *The History Teacher, 35,* 389–398.

This book is my contribution to this body of literature. It is a collection of history strategies and methods designed to heighten student interest that I developed first, as a ninth- and eleventh-grade history teacher in Washington DC and later, as a professor and director of social studies education at the college level and as a presenter and consultant on more than 60 Teaching American History Grants.

This is not a book of pedagogical theory. The reader will find that I have been sparse in my use of the terminology and jargon associated with the art of teaching. This is a book of ideas meant to jump-start and inspire teachers' own creativity. It is a book about making history fun and demystifying, not only the historical process but also the writing of history by uncovering the process for students in new and exciting forms. While there are abundant examples of lessons I have taught, my goal is to present these strategies and methods in a way that invites teachers of Grades 5–12 to develop their own creative lessons.

In developing these strategies, I have been highly influenced by the work of Theodore and Nancy Sizer. When I was a first year teacher, our academic dean selected Sizer's enlightening book *Horace's School* (1992) to be the focus of our summer institute.

To meet student needs more effectively, Sizer proposed, among other things, a restructuring of schools based on a clear vision of what skills, knowledge, and values a high school graduate would ideally need to reflect in order to function in a participatory democracy. Working on this model, he argued that schools should design a series of "exhibitions" that would enable students to display these qualities. Successful completion of the exhibitions, as opposed to academic hours or "seat time," he envisioned, would become the basis for a high school diploma. In addition, providing the resources and support that students need to perform well on such exhibitions would become the framework for the curriculum.

Inspired by Sizer's view of teaching, I decided to experiment with my own classes. I spent the better part of the last two weeks of summer thinking about how to apply what I had learned from Sizer and hoping that I could engage students on this level. Many of the teaching methodologies in this book grew out of those initial weeks of brainstorming and years of subsequent trial and error. A veteran teacher advised that I keep a journal my first year to be able to reflect on my teaching experiences the following summer. Fortunately, I took her advice. The journal was an indispensable ally in recalling some of the ideas and exchanges with students as I wrote this book.

HOW THIS BOOK IS ORGANIZED

Divided into six chapters, the book introduces six teaching methodologies and strategies. I begin with Haunted History in Chapter 1, a unique way to engage students in the study of the past through evidence of built environments and material culture. Chapter 2 illustrates how teachers can make their students agents of their own active learning by turning historical content into crime scenes, cases they must solve through the use of evidence and clues, much in the same way historians must piece together the past. Chapter 3 introduces a new way of having students look at primary and secondary sources using the forensic science of fingerprinting. Chapter 4 introduces the idea of the historical process in the intersection, the crossroads where the past takes shape. Chapter 5 discusses how to use court cases and legal dramas to engage students in the study of history. Finally, Chapter 6 borrows some of the language and techniques associated with the intriguing world of paranormal investigations for use with the study of history as a way to freshen up exercises. It further proposes introducing students to a formula that can help them organize their thoughts in thinking and writing about the past and its influence on the present.

To assist teachers in understanding and implementing the strategies I present, each chapter has the same basic structure. First I describe the strategy. Second, I explain how to implement it. Third I present examples of lessons I have taught using the strategy. At the end of each chapter are several reflection questions to help the reader think about implementing the methods covered in the chapter. Finally each chapter closes with a short list of resources available to help jumpstart the reader's use of the methods. Chapters 1, 2, 3 and 5 (on Haunted History, CSI, Historical Fingerprinting, and SCOTUS) include Web resources. The other chapters, on Historical Accident Reconstruction and ESP, do not lend themselves to Web resources and thus contain resources in the form of accessible books and articles. The grade levels of the lessons presented here range from middle to high school. I have tried to present them in a way that teachers in Grades 5–12 could easily adapt the grade-appropriate lessons to meet their needs as well.

Hopefully you will find much food for thought and inspiration in these pages in our never ending quest to make history come alive for our students.

REFERENCES

Bradley Commission on History in Schools. (1989). Building a history curriculum: Guidelines for teaching history in schools. *The History Teacher, 23*, 7–35.

National Council for History Education (Bradley Commission on History in Schools). (1988/2000). *Building a history curriculum: Guidelines for teaching history in schools.* Washington DC: Educational Excellence Network.

NEA conference declares civics challenge. (2003). Retrieved March 20, 2008, from http://www.cnn.com/2003/EDUCATION/07/03/students.history.ap/index.html

Sizer, T. (1992). *Horace's school: Redesigning the American high school.* Boston: Houghton Mifflin Company.

Wineburg, S. (2004). Crazy for history. *Journal of American History, 90*, 1413–1414.

1

Haunted History

Revealing the Hidden Past

Because someone is dead doesn't mean they're gone.

—Poster advertisement for the movie *Gothika* (2003)

History surrounds us in so many ways that it is often easy to ignore. From the eagle-eyed bronze statues that glare at us as we walk through the park, to the majestic and sometimes menacing memorials that command our attention from their roadside perches, to the names of the long dead and long forgotten who adorn the buildings, streets, and roads of our community, the past calls us to remember, and yet we do not.

In some places, the statues and historical markers are so numerous that they blend into the landscape. In other places, they appear so unexpectedly that we are somewhat startled as we come upon them. And should we stoop to notice the plaque peeking out at us from the underbrush or the statue mocking us from its overgrown nest, we might learn why they are there and what history they call us to remember.

Living and teaching in Washington DC in the mid 1990s, I found the city to be a treasure trove of forgotten but useful history. I concluded that having so much at my fingertips was a luxury I might not have anyplace else, so I made full use of the resources available in my teaching. Thinking back on my own primary and secondary education, I pondered how wonderful it would have been to study in a city where history is so much on display. Realizing how much my students took history for granted, I exhausted them with regular visits to the Smithsonian's National Portrait Gallery and the National Museum of American History. In my assignments, I challenged them to be super sleuths in investigating a historical figure in a photo or painting or even the artist or photographer of the work.

DISCOVERING HAUNTED HISTORY

It was on a field trip that I first discovered that the nation's capital, though steeped in history, was not unique and that there were other ways of getting students to appreciate the significance of the history that surrounds them. It was 7:30 in the morning on a sweltering September day in Washington DC in 1995. I boarded a bus with my eleventh grade students on a much anticipated trip to tour Frank Lloyd Wright's famous Fallingwater House in Pennsylvania, to be followed by an evening of camping and a day of white water rafting in scenic Ohiopyle State Park. Unfortunate enough to draw bus duty, I settled near the front, next to one of my sleeping students for the four-hour ride. After an hour or so the bus came alive with the familiar chatter of teens loosed from school.

By mid morning the students' euphoria was beginning to wane, as I made yet another tour of the bus. Toward the back, I sat down with three of my history students engaged in a game of the dozens, while another read quietly beside. The bus had pulled off the interstate into a little town so we could have lunch. In preparation for the trip, we had spent weeks in class talking about Frank Lloyd Wright and Edgar Kaufman Sr., for whom Wright had constructed Fallingwater House. I had also talked to my students about the devastating Johnstown flood that had struck on May 31, 1889, some sixty miles southwest of where the Wright house would later be built, and which claimed more than 2,209 lives in what, prior to Hurricane Katrina in 2005, was one of the worst natural disasters in United States history.

But I was surprised when one of my students, reading a state road sign giving the county name, playfully called out, "Hey Mr. Williams, who was Fayette?" The familiar game of stump the teacher was on. I suspected that Fayette County, Pennsylvania, was named for the famous Marquis de La Fayette, hero of both the American and French Revolutions, but unfamiliar with Pennsylvania history I played it cautious. "Oh," I said trying to be as matter of fact as possible, "I couldn't possibly tell you about that; I promised I would keep quiet." "Tell us about what?" another student inquired. "How the ghost of Fayette haunts this county," I responded, struggling to come up with something. Although I had prepared to tell the students ghost stories around the camp fire later that evening, obviously none of them were going to involve Fayette. Now the students were intrigued. I had their rapt attention. "Come on, Mr. Williams," they squealed with curious delight, "you have to tell us." "I promised the head-masters that I wouldn't tell you this story," I replied trying to appear firm and solemn while fighting back the urge to laugh. "You guys are far too young to handle it," I continued, "and besides none of you would sleep tonight if I told you." This response predictably set off a chorus of moans and protests. Some students were obviously spooked, but most were just curious. Wanting to preserve that curiosity and spare myself the grueling gauntlet of the eleventh-grade version of the third degree, I was well on my way to the front of the bus before they could plead their case.

That night we told ghost stories, but realizing I had a genuine teach-able moment, I stuck to my story about taking an oath of silence on Fayette, who I confirmed from one of the park staff was in fact Marie-Joseph-Paul-Yves-Roch-Gilbert du Motier, better known as the Marquis de La Fayette. I promised them, however, that I would reveal all I knew about the haunting if they discovered the origins of the county name. When we arrived home late Saturday evening, I began researching the Revolutionary War hero. But now I had to construct a story of my own. Why would La Fayette be "haunting" this county in Pennsylvania? One of the most intriguing figures of the American Revolution, the Marquis de La Fayette was named an honorary citizen of the United States, and his name, sans his title, was used in honor throughout the country. In fact, more than two dozen states from Alabama to Iowa to Utah have counties that bear his name.

On Monday morning my students showed up prepared to do battle. "We found Lafayette," one spoke up. "He wasn't even from Pennsylvania," he stated accusingly. "So why is he haunting the county?" I challenged. After several guesses the students were frustrated. Finally one young woman offered a possible explanation. "Maybe he's mad because we for-got him," she explained, "He actually did a lot for America." "Like what?" I pressed, curious to see how much she had learned about the life of the esteemed Frenchman. "Well," she said after a few moments, "he was really impressed with our struggle for independence, especially the part about the rights of man. He gave money to our cause, but most of all he came here to fight with General Washington and the Revolutionary Army even though this was not really his fight." "The Americans were so grateful," another student chimed in, reading hastily from notes she had taken on Lafayette, "Congress asked President Monroe to invite him back to the United States in 1824. He stayed for over a year visiting cities in all of the then 24 states. Congress even voted to pay him $200,000 for his services during the war, and they honored him by setting aside some land for a town to be named in his honor."

"What if anything does this tell you about the American Revolution?" I pressed them further.

"I now see what you meant when you said that Jefferson was not only writing to convince the colonists to support the revolution," one of the students spoke up in the back. "The Declaration of Independence helped to get the French on our side." He continued, "Even though they already did not like the British, it helped that they agreed with the ideas behind the revolution." After a few more minutes of discussion, I told the students I was giving everyone five extra credit points. They were, predictably, ecstatic. I was happy as well. It was, without question, one of the best exchanges I had had with my eleventh graders up until that point, and I was anxious to keep it going.

WHAT IS HAUNTED HISTORY?

The Lafayette exercise, which I dubbed Haunted History, quickly became one of my teaching staples. On the bulletin board of my classroom, I began posting HOST Files—HOST standing for Historically Opulent Subject Transparent, or really rich hidden history. These files provided clues couched in the form of questions about mysterious persons, places, or events. At first I offered extra credit for the first person to bring me the right answer, but soon I amended that to include the students who were able to demonstrate what they had learned in our bimonthly discussions on the HOST File subjects. In the beginning I remained pretty conventional, picking out names and subjects closely related to required course "coverage." For example, the HOST Files I covered in my teaching of the Age of Jackson included Peggy Eaton and the Petticoat War and the Trail of Tears.

By December, however, I was back to looking outside the classroom for inspiration, and the DC area did not disappoint. Every building, street sign, and historical marker offered the potential for new HOST Files, and I, quite frankly, was learning as much as my students about the rich history of the area through the street names, memorials, and plaques beckoning for recognition. After a while I realized that rather than my finding all the subjects for HOST Files, I should engage my students to ferret out the "ghosts" for themselves. Derived from the then-popular Japanese animé series *Gatchaman*, known as *G-Force* in the United States, a small band of my students were dubbed G-Force, or "ghost force," for their ghost-busting history skills. Instead of road games like "That's My Car," many of my students began ghost hunting, or HOST hunting as I called it (see Figure 1.1 for our HOST busting kit). There were even in-class competitions between the students in their quest to figure out why "certain people" or events in the form of memorials might be hanging around. I was constantly struck not only by their creativity but by how much they seemed to be learning unconnected to the textbook. I also never tired of the compliments from our librarian, who welcomed the endless stream of inquires coming from my classes.

FIGURE 1.1   What's in Your HOST Busting Kit?

- A person or event that connects national and local content
- A monument, marker, building or memorial that bears the person or event's name/dates
- A primary source or photograph that conveys the subject's ESP and larger historical significance
- Appropriate photographs or other images to convey a sense of mystery

In order to earn full credit, students not only had to identify the individual or place but also explain the historical significance behind it, whether actual, as in the case of Lafayette, or symbolic, as in the case of our school, which was named for the British philosopher Edmund Burke. It was my way of modeling cultural literacy for them by showing them how much more they could get out of not only my class, but their city, their state, and their whole lives by engaging with history (as noted in the Introduction). More important, I was allowing them to become historians searching for answers to questions with boundless possibilities for intellectual growth and self discovery. Last but not least, I was engaging my own intellectual curiosity and using my imagination to explore with my students the vast reservoir of historical content sitting in plain view. This was an important step in my own growth and development as a teacher. I found myself reading with keen interest the words of historian James Axtell (2001), who wrote of the need for history teachers to

> employ our imaginative faculties throughout the historical process because, as Logan Pearsall Smith once wrote to Virginia Woolf, "People only exist for us in our thoughts about them. They float like slow, strange fish in the . . . aquarium tanks of our imaginations." . . . [W]e must use our imaginations to reanimate the known facts and restore them to life, to fill the holes in our evidence with informed guesses, to reestablish, in the face of hindsight's certainties, the choices that the dead once enjoyed in the past, and to discern the larger forces that transcended and patterned the individual lives of our subjects. (p. 436)

Using an analytical tool I called ESP, I created an evidence review sheet specifically for Haunted History (see Figure 1.2). Playing on the idea of giving students a "sixth sense" about the past, I tied ESP to the categories most often found in content standards—economic, social, and political. Was the haunting economically motivated? Was it purely social, or could it be classified as a political haunting? (See Chapter 6 for a more complex use of ESP.) The more we engaged in the exercise, the less students were willing to ascribe a single cause to the haunting mysteries. In short, they had begun to think more like historians: unwilling to make their case in one area, they thoroughly exhausted all possibilities, usually settling on a combination of reasons rather than on a single factor.

FIGURE 1.2   Haunted History ESP Evidence Review Worksheet

- Who is the person or what was the event?
- What was the economic influence of the person or what were the economic consequences of the episode or event?
- What was the political influence of the person or what were the political consequences of the episode or event?
- What was the social significance of the person or what were the social consequences of the episode or event?
- What is the relationship of the person or event to your community and/or state?

Haunted History builds on the principles established in *Understanding by Design* (Wiggins & McTighe, 1998). Defined by allowing students to become the investigators and conduits for their own active learning, Haunted Histories, like the CSI Approach discussed in Chapter 2, can reinforce the importance of history as a means of connecting students to the wider community and also underscores their need to be engaged members of that community.

CONSTRUCTING HOST FILES

The key to designing meaningful Haunted History units is not to lose sight of the process of discovery. Use HOST Files to create challenging puzzles for the students, but be sure to provide them with enough clues and the proper tools to dig for the answer.

How to Begin

Select easily accessible sites that tie to state, local, and national content. Good sources for these types of sites are your state content standards. Most state standards include a list of performance indicators and terms, including the names of important people from the state who have helped shape the history of the nation. Sources for HOST Files can include

Plaques, monuments, and other memorials

Town names

Bridges

Historical actors

Battlefields

Warships

Famous residents

Famous or infamous events

Street and highway names

Building names including names of schools, government buildings, and hospitals

Names of parks and recreational areas

Places listed on the National Register of Historic Places

Paintings on public display

Sculptures

"Abandoned places" or rumored sites of historical significance

Sacred properties, including burial grounds and other sites that, while not popularly recognized as significant, may hold importance to a particular group of people in your community

HOST File Numbers and Clues

Once you select a subject for a case, or HOST File, give it a number. The HOST File case number is vital. It provides the first clue for students and reminds them of the importance of chronology. You can use the case number to reinforce chronology or emphasize important dates. The case number can be anything from the subject's birth and death years to a specific day, the date of an important event, or even the broad parameters of a historical era (e.g., the Gilded Age, 1865–1900). When possible, use dates that are themselves searchable especially if you plan to have students utilize the Internet in searching for the subject of your case. Here is an example from New Hampshire.

FIGURE 1.3

HOST File # 1874–1963

Since 1963 people have reported seeing an apparition of the rather scholarly looking gentleman pictured here (Figure 1.3), wildly roaming about the east side of Route 28 about 1.7 miles south of Derry, as if he were lost—a word that incidentally rhymes with his "chilly" name. Who is the former poet laureate who continues to haunt Derry, and why does he continue "stopping by the woods on a snowy evening" in search of "the road not taken"?

In the file text put all clues in italics or enclosed in quotation marks to set them apart from the rest of the text. In the same manner as the case number, the clues should also be searchable. With the Robert Frost example above, the names of his poems "Stopping by the Woods on a Snowy Evening" and "The Road Not Taken" are enclosed in quotation marks, as is the word "chilly." It is okay to include heuristic clues to help students practice making educated guesses based on minimal evidence.

Last but not least (and this is essential if your case is built around a place that students can visit), include clear directions that will put them in the vicinity without necessarily giving up the identity of the person or event.

Haunted History as Assessment Pieces

In *Engagement in Teaching History,* Drake and Nelson (2004) explain that performance assessment activities should reveal three dimensions of a student's historical literacy. These include (1) knowledge of historical facts, themes, and ideas; (2) the ability to reason illustrated by their ability to "analyze, evaluate, and synthesize historical evidence"; and (3) the ability to "communicate their knowledge and reasoning to a wider audience" (p. 117). With the proper planning, a carefully constructed Haunted History exercise can help you do all three.

- Use the file number and clues to encourage students to ask questions.
- Be broad in your use of chronology to encourage students to make connections that will require them to synthesize information and explain their rationale in making the connections.
- Think deeply about possible sources for your cases. Gerald Danzer and Mark Newman (1991) include built environments and folklore, folkways, and mythology among more traditional types of evidence (such as print documents, fine and graphic arts, and electronic media). Consider these as sources for Host files as well.

A SAMPLING OF HOST FILES

What follows are a few examples of Haunted Histories to serve as a guide to creating your own Haunted History files. One of the great things about Haunted Histories are that once created they can be easily shared among faculty members. Consider suggesting that every teacher in your unit submit a Haunted History to create a neat resource for your school or district. They can also be easily adapted to grade levels by altering the "clues" provided in the set up. Finally, yet importantly, remember to have fun!

HOST File #1851–1852–1887

For more than 50 years, residents of Glenwood, Colorado, have complained of seeing a disembodied dentist "Earping" about his presumed "Tombstone." What circumstances led to this "doc's" eternal "holiday?" Why is he not "O.K." with his final resting place? Lastly, how is this haunting connected to Valdosta, Georgia; the "white plague"; gambling; and the settlement of the Wild West?

I presented the above mystery to a professional development seminar of history and social studies teachers from Valdosta, Georgia, the original home of gunslinger John Henry "Doc" Holliday, who also appears in the state content standards. Note the local, state, and national content connections.

An investigation into Holliday's life portrays the complexity of historical analysis, succinctly laid out in the Bradley Commission's (1989) vital themes and habits of the mind (listed in the Introduction). A well-constructed Haunted History should allow students to practice a number of these habits as demonstrated in the example of "Doc" Holliday. In their quest to understand the significance of the past, the students will have to sift through the evidence, distinguishing between the important and the inconsequential. In addition, they will have to grapple with the forces of the nonrational, the irrational, and the accidental, all of which are well reflected in life of "Doc" Holliday.

Consider the "testimony" of Holliday's longtime friend Wyatt Earp, who tried to make sense out of Holliday's troubled existence: "He was a dentist, but he preferred to be a gambler. He was a Georgian, but preferred to be a frontiersman and a vagabond. He was a philosopher, but he preferred to be away. He was long, lean, ash blond and the quickest man with a six-shooter I ever knew."

In the West, we are told, restless women and men like Holliday found freedom to pursue their passions in the wilds of the frontier. What your students will uncover is that Holliday suffered from tuberculosis, also known as consumption or "the White Plague." He originally moved west in an attempt to ease the symptoms of this debilitating disease, continuing for a while his work as a dentist. This is a good way to get students developing the habit of mind "the often-tentative nature of judgments about the past" (Bradley Commission, 1989). It should also help them in recognizing the uncertain paths that individuals who have made a difference in history sometimes take. In the course of investigating the presumed haunting, students will also be uncovering the history of their own community in relation to the history of the nation. Encouraging them to interrogate the evidence they discover will enrich the experience. For example, why was there no treatment for the "White Plague"? How common was the disease? In what ways did it influence the lives of ordinary Americans?

HOST File # 07111804:
A Federalist Haunting in Weehawken

The New Jersey Historical Investigation Squad requests your help in identifying an event that took place over two hundred years ago, whose anniversary is on July 11, and which continues to haunt Weehawken, NJ, to this day. What happened there? How did it result in the "Burr"ial of the first president's "little lion," and how did it threaten to topple the careers of some of the most important men of the day? What is its ESP?

FIGURE 1.4

This example uses a combination of ESP and Haunted History to reinforce social studies content while taking advantage of a local history connection to historical content of national import. It also incorporates the use of "this day in history," engaging students through the use of a fun fact or historically significant tidbit related to the date. The ill-fated duel between sitting Vice President Aaron Burr and former President Washington's closet advisor and the nation's first Secretary of the Treasury, the little lion Alexander Hamilton, resulted in Hamilton's death. As was the custom of the day, Hamilton accepted a challenge from Burr to settle their political and personal differences on a field of honor in a duel. Presenting the duel and its outcome as a mystery allows students not only to uncover the social and political differences between these two highly influential men that led to the tragic contest, but also the social, economic, and political consequences of the clash and its lingering cultural significance—hence the language, "which continues to haunt Weehawken, NJ, to this day."

HOST File # 1644–1718–1987

Sometime in 1892, a photographer snapped the ominous image of the 26-ton behemoth pictured in Figure 1.5 near his "station" in center city. Rumored to have reached an agreement with the city from beyond the grave, the subject of this statue is said to have cursed the city for refusing to honor that agreement. Your mission, should you choose to accept it, is to help the Eagles win by identifying this "Giant Quaker" and author of the "Great Treaty," locate his hiding place amongst the clouds, and uncover his importance to Philadelphia and the nation before the end of the football season.

The subject is obviously the Pennsylvania colonial proprietor, William Penn. Most Philadelphia residents are familiar with the so-called curse of Billy Penn, which has been blamed for undermining efforts by

FIGURE 1.5

Source: Jeffrey M. Vinocur.

the city's professional sports teams to win a championship since the 76ers did so in 1983. It is a popular piece of folklore that most students could easily identify with and become excited about, thereby linking their study of history to their interest in sports. The curse itself dates back to an important event in the history of the city. In March of 1987 crews completed construction of One Liberty Place, officially making it the city's tallest building. The massive skyscraper exceeded the pinnacle of William Penn's statue perched atop Philadelphia's historic City Hall. This snub led to the curse, and hence the city's championship drought. This unit requires that students not only recognize William Penn and be able to say something about his accomplishments for the city, state, and nation, but also analyze and evaluate the evidence in light of the alleged curse. Finally they must give an explanation of the curse, or lack thereof, based on the evidence. The unit also allows them to better acquaint themselves with Philadelphia by actually doing history. The smaller pieces of information like the completion of city's tallest building tie in with more substantive ideas like the colony's founding and why its proprietor continues to be honored in public space.

This Haunted History is an excellent example of how teachers can demonstrate the importance of history beyond the narrow confines of the textbook, incorporating local history, national content, and a connection to public history that engages students in the history of their community and invites them to investigate that history with the ESP strategy.

Haunted History Priority File: "13 Ghosts"

Beginning in 1952 travelers began reporting sightings of 13 ghosts along New Jersey roadways. One ghost carries a shovel and is frequently seen hunching near the trees, another is seen hovering near Woodbridge Township and has a very special illuminating glow, while another in the same area has been known to whisper the name Stephen. One of the female "indomitable spirits" has been seen clutching a red cross. Your mission, should you choose to accept it, is to identify these 13 ghosts and establish their ESP to help put them to rest once and for all.

Anyone who has ever traveled the New Jersey Turnpike might recognize these as the 12 rest stops. The rest areas do not bear the full names of their honorees, such as Thomas Woodrow Wilson, but their names as they were popularly known in life, like Woodrow Wilson. Many teachers and New Jersey residents have joined me in the admission that for years they assumed that #8 Joyce Kilmer was a woman. In fact, Alfred Joyce Kilmer was a famous poet who was selected because many think that one of his most celebrated poems, "Trees," was written about the trees of the Garden State. Given the range of personalities and historical periods covered here, one could almost teach United States history through New Jersey's rest stops. Note the names and dates of the persons honored below. For teachers in the Northeastern Corridor whose students have likely traveled or will travel the famous roadway, this is a great example of Haunted History at work.

New Jersey's 13 "HOSTS"

- Clara Barton, 1821–1912, Civil War, Medicine, the Red Cross
- John Fenwick, 1618–1683, Colonial America. Fenwick founded the Salem, New Jersey, Quaker settlement known as Fenwick's Colony.
- Walt Whitman, 1819–1892, Gilded Age, Literature
- James Fenimore Cooper, 1789–1851, Antebellum America, Literature
- Richard Stockton, 1730–1781, The American Revolution, Signer of the Declaration of Independence
- "Thomas" Woodrow Wilson, 1856–1924, Progressive Era, the Presidency (see Figure 1.6)
- Molly Pitcher, The American Revolution
- "Alfred" Joyce Kilmer, 1886–1918, Progressive Era, Conservation
- Thomas Edison, 1847–1931, Gilded Age, Technology
- "Stephen" Grover Cleveland, the Gilded Age
- Alexander Hamilton, the Early Republic
- Vince Lombardi, the late 1950s and early 1960s
- You decide

FIGURE 1.6

Source: Library of Congress.

The 13th Ghost

Immediately most teachers and students note that there are only 12 rest stops in New Jersey and inquire about New Jersey's 13th HOST. The reference to 13 ghosts is meant to elicit connection with the movie of the same name. But it also opens up the possibility for students to explore the work of the public historian. By asking students to consider who should be included in the unlikely event of a new rest stop on the New Jersey Turnpike, teachers provide their students with the opportunity to explore questions essential to the writing of history such as, "What is important and what is not?" It also allows them to explore the history of New Jersey and its connection to the nation in the context of deciding what other contributions state residents have made to the history of the United States.

While not every state is blessed with named rest stops like New Jersey, there are other ways to apply this strategy in situations that allow students to evaluate the economic, social, and political contributions of persons in history; weigh the evidence; and make decisions about whether they should be honored in a public space. For example, every state contributes two statues to the Capitol in Washington DC in honor of its most prominent citizens. Using these as a starting point, the motivated history teacher could craft a year-long series of HOST Files related not only to these figures but also to people who might be haunting other corners of the state demanding that they too be represented. Teachers wishing to take this approach can begin by accessing the Web site of the National Statuary Hall Collection in the United States Capitol, which can be found at http://www.aoc.gov/cc/art/nsh/index.cfm. If you are planning a trip to Washington DC or your state capitol, Haunted History opens up additional opportunities to engage your students in the study of history while getting them to think and ask questions like social scientists through an exercise that is as fun as it is enlightening.

QUESTIONS FOR REVIEW AND REFLECTION

1. Take a few minutes to think about some of the statues, monuments, and historical markers that exist in your own community. Would any of these make good Haunted History Files? As you are thinking, grab a pen and write down the ones you might make use of in creating your own HOST files.

2. Comb your state content standards and/or perform a quick Internet search for local historical figures or events from your area. Are there any monuments or markers to these in proximity to where you teach? How might you use Haunted History to engage students in the study of this important local history?

3. Are you aware of any local legends or folklore of a historical nature associated with your city or state? How might you use Haunted History to help your students distinguish between myth and fact using that local history as a vehicle?

4. Are there any buildings, roadways, or schools near you that bear the name of historical figures or events? If so, whom or what are they named for? Can you think of a historical figure that should be represented but is not? Using your state content standards as guide, consider creating a list of forgotten souls for your students to investigate as part of a semester-long project to learn more about the community. Toward the close of the semester, consider having your students vote and then draft a petition project to christen some yet unnamed public space for the person they found to be most significant.

REFERENCES

Axtell, J. (2001). The pleasures of teaching. *The History Teacher, 34*, 433–446.

Bradley Commission on History in Schools. (1989). Building a history curriculum: Guidelines for teaching history in schools. *The History Teacher, 23*, 7–35.

Danzer, G. A. & Newman, M. (1991). *Tuning in: Primary sources in the teaching of history.* Chicago: The World History Project.

Drake, F. & Nelson, L. (2004). *Engagement in teaching history.* Upper Saddle River, NJ: Pearson.

Wiggins, G. & McTighe, J. (1998). *Understanding by design.* Alexandria, VA: Association for Supervision and Curriculum Development.

RESOURCES AND FURTHER READING

Boland, B. M. (2002). Historic places: Common ground for teachers and historians. *Magazine of History, 16(2)*, 19–21.

Written by a historian with the National Park Service (NPS), this article on the NPS's Teaching with Historic Places initiative is a great place to begin to stimulate your thinking about how to engage historic places as both an important part of historical memory and a tool for teaching. The essay can also be found online from the Web site of the *OAH Magazine of History*, retrieved March 20, 2008, from http://www.oah.org/pubs/magazine/publichistory/boland.html

Egan, K. (1989). Layers of historical understanding. *Theory and Research in Social Education, 17*, 280–294.

This great article proposes that teachers consider different ways of presenting historical information in an effort not only to pique student curiosity but also to address different student learning styles and developmental levels. In addition to contributing useful categories of history, Eagan also encourages engaging students' imaginations in the study of history. Haunted History can be used in conjunction with much of what is discussed by Egan.

Fleming, T. (1999). *Duel: Alexander Hamilton, Aaron Burr, and the future of America.* New York: Basic Books.

Far from light reading, this most recent treatment of the Burr–Hamilton duel is comprehensive in scope and looks at consequences of the duel for the nation as a whole. This would be a good choice for summer reading, but in building your Haunted History or Cold Case and determining the long-term impact of the shooting, the last two chapters will suffice.

Gabella, M. S. (1994). Beyond the looking glass: Bringing students into the conversation of historical inquiry. *Theory and Research in Social Education, 22*, 340–363.

This stimulating article posits that true reform in curriculum instruction will require a fundamental shift away from the teacher and text as the sole authoritative voice toward a model of instruction that represents a co-investigation by teacher and student on a path of historical discovery. Haunted History investigations encourage this type of teaching.

Gillespie, A. & Rockland, M. A. (1989). *Looking for America on the New Jersey Turnpike.* New Brunswick: Rutgers University Press.

This attractive book is a great place to start if you are interested in the history of the New Jersey Turnpike and also in exploring ways to use roadways and other named public space in your own community to create your own Haunted History files.

Hamer, D. (1998). *History in urban places: The historic districts of the United States.* Columbus: Ohio State University Press.

This study is very useful, especially for teachers in urban areas interested in researching aspects of their own community history. This book is also a great resource for thinking about unconventional sources of history in your midst.

Linder, S. A. (1998). When the dealing's done: John H. (Doc) Holliday and the evolution of a western myth. *Journal of the West, 37(2):* 53–60.

This is a good article to build background content knowledge on Doc Holiday. It is also very useful for its discussion of how myths evolve and how you might apply this in creating Haunted History files related to historical content where you live or teach. This would be a good source to use in conjunction with the Egan article cited here that also engages the use of myth in teaching history.

Moss, R. W. (2005). *Historic sacred places of Philadelphia.* Philadelphia: University of Pennsylvania Press.

This is a terrific resource for potential Haunted Histories for teachers living in or planning to visit the Philadelphia area. It is also a great resource for stimulating your own thinking about "sacred" places in your own city or state that you could mine for similar cases.

Pearce, J. N. (1999). Enduring friendship: James Monroe, Thomas Jefferson, James Madison and Lafayette. *Northern Neck of Virginia Historical Magazine, 49:* 5810–5819.

Although the journal may be somewhat difficult to come by, this is an excellent student-friendly article for those interested in adapting the Lafayette Haunted History exercise.

Pendleton, A. S. Jr. & Thomas, S. M. (1973). Doc Holliday's Georgia background. *Journal of Arizona History, 14(3),* 185–204.

This interesting article on Holiday is useful for demonstrating ways to link historic figures back to your community. It's not a how-to by any means, but if you have the time it is definitely worth a quick review.

Unger, H. G. (2002). *Lafayette.* New York: Wiley.

This lengthy but engaging study of Lafayette is a good book to add to your summer reading list if you are really captivated by the life and times of the Marquis.

On the Web

Architect of the Capitol. (n.d.). *The National Statuary Hall Collection.* Retrieved March 20, 2008, from http://www.aoc.gov/cc/art/nsh/index.cfm

The National Statuary Hall Collection is an excellent place to begin to look for subjects for your Haunted History files. Each state contributes two statues. Consider using these as the subjects for your first Haunted History Files or as a platform to have students uncover other historical figures from your state that should replace them.

National Park Service. (n.d.). *History and culture: For teachers.* Retrieved March 20, 2008, from http://www.nps.gov/history/teachers.htm

Updated regularly and full of useful content, the National Parks Service provides a plethora of materials for teachers. The site also includes an excellent link full of suggestions for teaching with museum collections, another good source for HOST Files. Definitely make this one of your stops in thinking about creating your own Haunted History cases.

National Park Service. (n.d.). *The National Register of Historic Places.* Retrieved March 20, 2008, from http://www.nps.gov/nr/

Partnered with the National Park Service, the Web site of the National Register of Historic Places is a wonderful resource for identifying historically significant properties in your area around which to build your Haunted History cases.

Public Broadcasting System. (2000). *American Experience: The Duel.* Retrieved March 20, 2008, from http://www.pbs.org/wgbh/amex/duel/

If you are looking for Web materials on the Burr–Hamilton duel, look no further than PBS's celebrated American Experience site. With clips, a timeline, maps and a wonderful teacher's guide, this is a quick and accessible resource with all the materials you need to build your Haunted History file.

2

The CSI Approach

Making Students Detectives

Indeed, history is nothing more than a tableau of crimes and misfortunes.

—Voltaire (1694–1778)

L ong before the CBS television show *CSI* graced the airways, I devised a derivative of "crime scene investigator" into what would ultimately develop as Content Scene Interpreter, or the CSI Approach. My interest in presenting "history" like a crime scene grew partly out of my use of mock trials (see Chapter 5) and partly out of my students' fascination with forensic science. My eleventh graders, in particular, were delighted with one of my colleagues in the biology department who used forensics to promote student participation and interest in science research. At least that is how he explained it. My students simply thought it was cool; nevertheless, I genuinely admired how much they talked about what they were learning in the course. Sending my students to investigate "haunted" historical sites was still fun, but I wondered if I could adapt the forensics methodology in a modified format to have them uncover history. The crime scene scenario presented the greatest possibilities. First, my students' interest was already piqued by their science class. Second, the idea of having them investigate history, to interrogate sources rather than simply read and regurgitate them, was exciting to me.

Certainly it was not new to conceptualize the role of the historian as a kind of detective, time traveling through the ages through the use and interrogation of documents, photographs, and other artifacts to uncover the past. Historians James West Davidson and Mark Lytle (1982) provide numerous examples of how the work of the historian parallels that of the eagle-eyed detective, carefully poring over and weighing the evidence associated with some event in the process of providing the most plausible explanation for what took place. Particularly exciting was their presentation of history as a process of discovery through trial and error. Their absorbing presentation of the rise and fall of Connecticut patriot Silas Deane as a historical mystery, for example, became a model for how I engaged students, not only in the reading of primary sources but in asking questions and interrogating those sources. Knowing what questions to ask, when to ask them, and how to ask them was only one part of the process. Understanding how to shape them into a narrative was the other. I began to think seriously about how to get my students to think and process information like historical detectives. The methods used in the CSI Approach were my vehicle.

WHAT IS THE CSI APPROACH?

My students were most familiar with the traditional model of middle and high school social studies and history instruction, which I followed as a new teacher. I introduced a topic with readings, lectured on it, and engaged the students in a brief discussion, before having them regurgitate information back to me on a test or in essay form. My assessments usually took the standard framework of explaining the causes or consequences of some event. In contrast, with the CSI Approach, I endeavored to have them unearth history as time-traveling detectives on a mission to explain the past. When I first used CSI, we had just begun our discussion of Jim Crow segregation and the Progressive movement. I decided to build my first "Cold Case" around a compelling episode from the period to test my students' receptiveness. In previous years, I had intrigued my students with the story of Ota Benga, an African Pygmy who was placed on display in the Bronx Zoo in 1906 and committed suicide ten years later. The story itself was enough to draw their attention.

A Tale of Tragedy

Ota Benga was a member of a forest tribe of small stature caught up in tribal warfare inspired by European political intrigue in his native Congo. His family was killed, and he was taken captive. Eventually sold to South Carolina missionary and explorer Samuel Phillips Verner, who had come to the region in search of "pygmies" to exhibit at the St. Louis Exposition (1904), Benga assisted Verner in recruiting other natives to come to the United States to stage what Verner billed as an authentic representation of African village life.

When the exposition ended, Benga returned with Verner to Africa, where he spent the next 18 months assisting the explorer in his "research." When Verner returned to the United States in 1906, he brought Benga with him to New York. Under financial strain, Verner returned to South Carolina to try to raise funds to continue his work. He left Benga in the care of the director of the American Museum of Natural History.

Assuming that Benga might be more comfortable somewhere similar to what museum staff perceived to be his native habitat, and sensing an opportunity, Benga's caretaker turned him over to William T. Hornaday, the director of the Bronx Zoo. Hornaday promptly placed Benga on display in the monkey house with an orangutan and a gorilla, billing the four foot eleven man "The African Pigmy," as the missing link between humanity and the ape. After a storm of protest from the African American community, Hornaday eventually agreed to end the exhibit.

For a brief time life improved for Benga. Entrusted to the care of the "colored" orphanage in Brooklyn, he learned to speak English and made friends. Unable to shake the shadow of his time at the zoo, in 1910 he relocated to Lynchburg, VA, where he became a Christian and enrolled in a local seminary. Within a few years, however, he grew increasingly despondent. He often talked of returning home, but as a lowly day laborer first on a local plantation and later in a tobacco factory, he was unable to save up enough money. After struggling with depression, he took his own life in March of 1916. (Bradford & Blume, 1992)

I had typically included the tragic account of Benga's life and death as part of our discussion of *Plessy v. Ferguson,* Jim Crow, and race and eugenics in the late 19th and early 20th centuries. In explaining the birth of state-sanctioned segregation that was Jim Crow, I used the account of Ota Benga to demonstrate how white racial attitudes envisioned people of African descent as subhuman, while I highlighted the ways in which people of African descent challenged these classifications. Looking to have students uncover the history on their own, I decided to turn the Benga account into a crime scene.

Cold Case # 1906

In the summer of 1906, the Bronx Zoo in New York was the scene of a curious exhibit (some called it a crime against humanity) that at its peak attracted some 40,000 visitors a day. What was on display in the famed monkey house at the zoo? How did it cost the zoo's director one of his "friends" and how did the troubling spectacle eventually help to put "Darwinian" theory on trial? Given your knowledge of U.S. history up to this point, how could this have happened in the cradle of liberty?

As a source, I provided my students with copies of three 1906 newspaper articles from the *New York Times* that chronicled Benga's stay at the zoo and the firestorm of controversy it ignited (African Pygmy, 1906; Bushman, 1906; Man and monkey, 1906; all three articles are reprinted in Williams, 2003). In crafting their account of the incident, they had to find two additional pieces of evidence including at least one primary source.

The purpose of the exercise was not merely to acquaint students with the life of Ota Benga or to hone their research skills in finding out more about him, but to have them play the role of historians in explaining why he came to reside in the monkey house at the Bronx Zoo. Since this was my first attempt, I equipped my students with some training wheels, telling them that their explanation at the very least should include social, economic, cultural, and political factors that may have led to Benga's predicament. They could only declare their case file closed after considering how the things they discovered offered a coherent explanation for Benga's tenure at the zoo. Part of the process, of course, was deciding what to include and what to leave out. In order to get full credit, they had to consider the totality of Benga's experience in relation to the actions of those around him. Benga's trip to the zoo began long before he arrived in New York and involved both United States and European history.

I asked my students to refrain from making a final determination about the actions of the various people involved without first considering their motivations and second backing up their conclusions with evidence from the crime "content" scene. They could not label the director of the zoo as a "bad person" without exploring his actions and motivations in consigning Benga to the monkey house. Although he did a terrible thing, William T. Hornaday considered himself a man of science. Until his decision to place Benga in the zoo, Hornaday was a positive mover and shaker in the world. A conservationist, he was instrumental in the foundation of the Smithsonian Museum and the National Zoo in Washington DC. He also believed in evolution, and as a supporter of live animal preserves, which inspired him to create the National Zoo, he decided to place Ota Benga in his presumed natural habitat among the apes. The arguments of the African American leaders in their demand that Benga be released squarely put social darwinism on trial.

In developing the CSI Approach, I drew on the ideas of Grant Wiggins and Jay McTighe (1998) in their book *Understanding by Design*. They encourage educators to "think like assessors, not activity designers" (p. 63). When teachers begin thinking like assessors, these authors observe, they actually plan backward—designing assessments based on what they want students to know before they plan their learning sequence. This process of backward planning, they concluded, can help teachers assess whether their students are meeting the objectives the teachers have designed for them.

Built on this backward planning model, the CSI Approach helps teachers assess both skills and content in a way that is fun and engaging for the students. Treating historical content like evidence at a crime scene opens up opportunities for teachers to reinforce skill sets while teaching content. In constructing my own CSI units, I consistently remind myself of five principal goals I want the exercise to accomplish. Students should be able to

1. Interrogate the sources.

2. Explore and evaluate alternative viewpoints from a variety of secondary sources, most important, the work of other historians.

3. Hunt for additional evidence.

4. Make an argument based on the evidence.

5. Defend their position.

CONSTRUCTING COLD CASES

Studying the past is a lot like detective work. Therefore every primary source should be treated like evidence at a crime scene. The key is the presentation of the document. CSI is a student-centered approach that uses primary source documents to teach American history.

CSI exercises can run the gamut from detailed units to homework assignments. If you want to give your students a little research assignment for homework, Cold Cases make great activities. They work well as library exercises or for small group work. An Alabama teacher created mini CSI investigations for all of the historically significant Alabamans in her content standards. A New York teacher chose to model her history Cold Cases on women in United States history. A New Jersey teacher decided to use CSI to ask his students to decide on the age-old question from the Gilded Age: Were the corporate titans that emerged after the Civil War "robber barons" or "captains of industry"?

How to Begin

To get started with the CSI Approach, follow these steps in constructing a Cold Case:

1. Identify a person or event of both local and national import.

2. Establish the ESP of the person or event.

3. Select primary sources to serve as evidence for your case (see Chapter 1 for a list of source suggestions).

4. Correlate your findings with your state content standards.

5. Begin building your case.

The remaining three steps are the same as in constructing a HOST File:

6. Use the case number to reinforce chronology and dates.

7. Choose images that convey a sense of the ESP of the person or event (which helps to reinforce critical thinking).

8. Find ways to work in additional content through analysis and review.

As with Haunted History, the best place to begin is with your state content standards. I have been pleasantly surprised by the number of teachers who have sent me copies of their Cold Cases featuring a variety of colorful characters appearing in their state standards and performance indicators.

After content standards, historiographical controversies are always a good choice for Cold Cases. They allow your students to evaluate not only primary source evidence but also secondary source material that they must take into consideration before arriving at a conclusion. For example, I selected Bacon's rebellion and its historiographical controversy and prepared the following Cold Case for my eleventh-grade AP students.

Cold Case # 1676

In the summer of 1676 the "pork chop" noble pictured in Figure 2.1 led a rebellion against Virginia's royal government. Was Bacon's Rebellion a precursor to the American Revolution? Or was it simply a food fight between two powerful and greedy rivals that only ended when one succumbed to the bloody flux? You decide.

After introducing the CSI in class, I assigned brief selections from two major works on Bacon's Rebellion:

- *The Governor and the Rebel* by Wilcomb E. Washburn (1972)
- *Torchbearer of the Revolution* by Thomas J. Wertenbaker (1940/ 1965)

FIGURE 2.1

Source: Library of Congress.

Each offers a radically different interpretation of Bacon's Rebellion and its meaning. The following day we discussed the student findings in their investigation.

Current events may also occasionally contribute a content rich crime scene. Take, for example, the Masaoka case included later in this chapter.

Finally, yet importantly, be creative and have fun. Exercises like CSI should be as enjoyable for you as for the students. Find ways to engage areas of history that make good mysteries but also make good sense in terms of your own research and interest. As with Haunted History, consider having your colleagues create a bank of CSI Cold Cases for your school based on your state content standards, important people from your town, and significant people of national import. This could make a great resource for your school and promote history in a fun and exciting format.

The Difference Between Haunted History and CSI

While Haunted History and CSI appear quite similar, there are some important differences. First, as much as possible, I tried to link HOST Files to physical places that the students could presumably go and visit, either in person or in cyberspace, including buildings, sculptures, memorials, and monuments.

Documents, however, are the primary focus of the Cold Cases in CSI. Presented with a problem or a historiographical dilemma, students are encouraged to ask questions and then to offer a possible answer or solution through interrogating the sources, accessing prior knowledge, carefully examining the image, and poring over the clues in each case. Simply identifying the subject of the Cold Case is not enough. The whole point is for them to explain what happened and why it happened. Students exhibit what they have learned rather than simply reproducing what they found. Here is a comparison of descriptions of Warren Harding as a CSI Cold Case and as a Haunted History HOST File. Note the subtle but important differences in presentation.

Cold Case #1923

After playing six rounds of golf in Vancouver, BC, a few days before, on a sunny day in August 1923 the dapper Ohioan pictured in Figure 2.2 died while holed up in a San Francisco hotel. Although acknowledged as a gifted speaker who spoke fluent "Gamalielese," no words could save him. What was churning in his belly that would make a promised "return to normalcy" for the nation impossible following his untimely demise, and why was his successor so curiously cool and "silent" about the whole sordid business?

HOST File #821923

In the midst of numerous scandals, the somber man pictured in Figure 2.2 once lamented, probably holding his "Teapot Dome," "I have no trouble with my enemies. I can take care of my enemies in a fight. But my friends, my goddamned friends, they're the ones who keep me walking the floor at nights!" Within a few months, he died under mysterious circumstances. More than 80 years later, some people claim that WGH continues to "walk the floors" especially near the roads of Blooming Grove, Ohio. Could he still be looking for his "Ohio Gang" or perhaps even a newspaper bearing his name, or are there other ESP-able reasons why #29 continues to haunt the Buckeye state?

FIGURE 2.2

Source: Library of Congress.

With the Cold Cases, students should engage the larger history of a period or era in relation to the subject. While the subject is the focal point of their inquiry, when they finish, they should be able to say something substantive about the period in which the person lived or that the event took place and place it in its larger historical context. For example, Ota Benga would be placed within European and American imperialism, Jim Crow segregation, eugenics and scientific racism, and social darwinism. With Haunted History, the subject's link to a landmark or memorial is crucial, since the main point is to stimulate students thinking about the history that surrounds them every day and the contributions that people from their own states have made to it.

A SAMPLING OF COLD CASES

Cold Case #1867–1934

After 17 years of success dispensing "Brad's drink," in 1923, this mannerly pill broker was robbed of his "pep" due to circumstances beyond his control. Who or what put "sugar" in his gas tank causing his successful enterprise to fizzle out and leaving him with a bad case of "dyspepsia"? Was it World War I, the Stock Market Crash, the Great Depression, or something far more sinister?

Ideally, one would want to use CSI to help students connect the meaning and importance of certain people and events over time in order to suggest cause–effect relationships and make comparisons. The Cold Case above, developed as part of a project for North Carolina, related to State Competency Goal 9: Prosperity and Depression (1919–1939) for eleventh and twelfth graders. It stated, "The learner will appraise the economic, social, and political changes of the decades of 'The Twenties' and 'The Thirties.'" It further asked that students be able to

1. Elaborate on the cycle of economic boom and bust in the 1920s and 1930s.

2. Analyze the extent of prosperity for different segments of society during this period.

3. Analyze the significance of social, intellectual, and technological changes of lifestyles in the United States.

This Cold Case connects the history of the United States, North Carolina, the First World War, and the Great Depression in an attractive story to which both teachers and students could relate. Furthermore, in its broad scope it touched on each of the indicators related to the state competency goal. The "mannerly pill broker" in the Cold Case was pharmacist Caleb Bradham, the creator and founder of Pepsi Cola. His story neatly parallels the nation's ills (no pun intended) and success from 1890 to 1930.

The Story of Pepsi

Born in New Bern, North Carolina, Caleb Bradham stumbled upon the formula for Pepsi-Cola while mixing up a cure for "dyspepsia," or indigestion, in the summer of 1893. Known as Brad's drink, for nearly five years it was available locally in North Carolina. Soon Bradham began to speculate about the possibilities of reaching a larger national market. With increased rail service, he postulated he could make the business a success. In order to make his product more marketable and competitive in 1898, he renamed his creation Pepsi Cola after the pepsin and cola nuts used in the recipe. That same year, he shrewdly purchased the trade name "Pep Cola" for $100 from a rival soft drink maker in Newark, New Jersey, whose business had failed.

Encouraged by the enthusiastic response of his customers, in 1902 Bradham began bottling the soft drink in the storeroom of his pharmacy. In 1903, Bradham paid a local artist to create the first Pepsi logo. On June 16 of that year, Bradham trademarked the name Pepsi Cola and soon after issued ninety-seven shares of stock for his new company Pepsi. For nearly two decades, Pepsi remained competitive in the soft drink market. Bradham, however, eventually lost the company by speculating on sugar prices during World War I. He assumed, in spite of fluctuations, that sugar prices would continue to rise. Instead they plummeted, leaving the hapless pharmacist

(Continued)

(Continued)

with an overpriced sugar supply. Bradham eventually went bankrupt, but not before selling the Pepsi trademark for $35,000 in 1923.

Over the next five years the company changed owners four times, eventually going bankrupt again in 1928. In 1931, the Loft Candy Company acquired Pepsi Cola. Loft president Charles G. Guth experimented with the formula, but success eluded him. Frustrated he even drafted a proposal to sell Pepsi to its chief competitor, the Coca-Cola Company. Coke, however, was not interested. After acquiring majority shares in the company, in 1934 Guth engineered an important reversal of Pepsi's fortunes when he authorized bottlers to sell twice the amount of Pepsi, a full twelve ounces, for the same price Coca-Cola and other soft drink manufacturers were charging for six ounces. At the height of the Great Depression, this set the soft drink apart from its competition.

In 1939 the company appeared in peril again, after the board of directors removed Guth for his competing interest in a rival cola. Not all was lost, however, due in large part to the vision of the company's newly minted president, Walter S. Mack.

A firm believer in marketing and promotion, Mack believed that the key to Pepsi's continued success lay in the new medium of radio advertising. In 1940 sales soared after a commercial for Pepsi became the first advertising jingle to be broadcast nationally. The jingle, "Nickel, Nickel," celebrated the favorable cost comparison of Pepsi to her rivals, twice the cola for the same price. The jingle became a smash hit, eventually being recorded in more than fifty languages. This stroke of advertising genius shored up the company's fortunes, helping her surge ahead of the competition. Pepsi remains a corporate giant to this day.

Although North Carolina's Competency Goal only asked that students demonstrate content knowledge through 1939, one aspect of CSI is to always try to emphasize a historical event's connection to the present. Clearly, the Pepsi Corporation's continued dominance in the soft drink market makes this Cold Case an attractive example for helping students to understand not only the period 1890–1930 but also its relationship to today. Students can see how innovations like the railroads and radio advertising influenced businesses in the early twentieth century as much as new forms of transportation and advertising such as the Internet influence business in our own day. Students also learn how government oversight and market issues influence society more broadly. All of these things affected Pepsi both negatively and positively in its growth and development as a corporation.

The Pepsi CSI demonstrates the importance of shaping your "content scene" in such a way as to encourage students to interrogate the facts. The questions in each CSI are designed to force students to confront alternative possibilities. If Bradham truly lost Pepsi due to fluctuations in sugar prices, for example, what caused those fluctuations? More important, were any of the circumstances leading up to fall of Braham attributable to other social, economic, political, or cultural phenomena at the time?

In looking at the content standards, I want students to see Pepsi as a triumph of science and technology as much as the individual will of its creator and other individuals like Guth and Mack who contributed to its success. In order to analyze the significance of social, intellectual, and technological changes of lifestyles in the United States related to the rise of Pepsi, the student has to appreciate Bradham's role as a pharmacist and how his experimentation and new technology, first the railroad and later the motor car, made his product accessible to a much larger market.

Cold Case #2000

During the summer of 2000, a fierce debate erupted over the proposed inclusion of a creed written by the debonair chap pictured in Figure 2.3 on the Japanese American World War II Memorial. While he spent his entire life working to promote the cause of Japanese rights, specifically as a leader of the Japanese American Citizens League, the oldest Asian American civil rights organization (founded in 1929), by the time of his death in 1991, many of his actions during the Second World War had severely tainted his legacy. Your challenge, should you choose to accept it, is to discover why.

FIGURE 2.3

Source: Courtesy of the J. Willard Marriott Library, University of Utah.

Based on the life of Japanese American civil rights activist Mike M. Masaoka, this Cold Case engages the legacy of Japanese immigration restrictions before and after the Second World War as well as how Japanese Americans dealt with discrimination. The document referred to in the case was Masaoka's Japanese American Creed, as read before the U.S. Senate and printed in the *Congressional Record* May 9, 1941. I became aware of the controversy over its inclusion in the war memorial from an August 2000 article in *Asian Week* (Hanley, 2000).

As you read the creed, note the wonderful points of comparison between Masaoka and Black civil rights leaders like Booker T. Washington and Martin Luther King Jr. Despite his efforts to promote civil rights, some condemned Masaoka for the timing and the tone of his speech, which according to many endorsed the internment of Japanese Americans during the Second World War. My students were quick to compare elements of his speech to Booker T. Washington's Atlanta Exposition Speech in 1895, in which Washington, claiming to speak for the masses of Black Americans, acquiesced to Jim Crow segregation in exchange for the promise of economic opportunity. Later on in the speech, however, Masaoka sounds very much like Martin Luther King Jr. In pleading for the acceptance of Japanese Americans as American citizens, Masaoka expressed, as the Reverend Dr. King would 22 years later in his "I have a dream" speech, the desire to live in a nation "where they will not be judged by the color of their skin but by the content of their character."

The Japanese American Creed

I am proud that I am an American citizen of Japanese ancestry, for my very background makes me appreciate more fully the wonderful advantages of this Nation. I believe in her institutions, ideals, and traditions; I glory in her heritage; I boast of her history; I trust in her future. She has granted me liberties and opportunities such as no individual enjoys in this world today. She has given me an education befitting kings. She has entrusted me with the responsibilities of the franchise. She has permitted me to build a home, to earn a livelihood, to worship, think, speak, and act as I please—as a free man equal to every other man.

Although some individuals may discriminate against me, I shall never become bitter or lose faith, for I know that such persons are not representative of the majority of the American people. True, I shall do all in my power to discourage such practices, but I shall do it in the American way—above board, in the open, through courts of law, by education, by proving myself to be worthy of equal treatment and consideration. I am firm in my belief that American sportsmanship and attitude of fair play will judge citizenship and patriotism on the basis of action and achievement, and not on the basis of physical characteristics.

Because I believe in America and I trust she believes in me, and because I have received innumerable benefits from her, I pledge myself to do honor to her at all times and in all places; to support her constitution; to obey her laws; to respect her flag; to defend her against all enemies, foreign or domestic; to actively assume my duties and obligations as a citizen, cheerfully and without any reservations whatsoever, in the hope that I may become a better American in a greater America.

Source: The Japanese American Creed by Mike Masaoka, read before the U.S. Senate, printed in the *Congressional Record* May 9, 1941, and submitted to the House Select Committee Investigating National Defense Migration.

Cold Case #9131857

The "Snavely" gentleman is credited with building "the sweetest place on earth." Even during the Great Depression it was rumored that "milk and honey" flowed through the "Chocolate and Cocoa Avenues" near his "High Point Mansion." However, shortly after the death of his beloved "Kitty" in 1915, he was involved in a transaction that left many questioning his intellectual "nougat." What led them to this conclusion? And, what role, if any, did the "saucy" boys he was known to surround himself with play? Why might he be accused of paying too much attention to the "Gospel" according to Carnegie?

In Pennsylvania, as in many other states, the content standards and performance indicators include the names of persons of historical import from the state who might make good subjects for CSI files. One such person is confectioner Milton Hershey. In addition to being a brilliant candy maker and astute business person, Hershey was also a great humanitarian. After the death of his beloved wife Catherine, known as "Kitty," he donated his entire fortune to establish a home and school for boys who had lost one or both of their parents. In tune with the prevailing ideas regarding education of his day, the Hershey school emphasized hard work as the key to individual success. All of the boys admitted to the school performed work for the company, such as milking the dairy cows, and were expected to learn a trade on a path to becoming responsible and productive members of society. In this sense Hershey is a great mirror of the ideals of the Gilded Age and Progressive era when Horatio Alger tales emphasized that any boy could make a success of himself by working hard and living a moral and upstanding life. Like many wealthy men of his day, most notably U.S. Steel founder Andrew Carnegie, Hershey was a firm believer in the Gospel of Wealth, the moral obligation of the rich to give back to those less fortunate than themselves. As Carnegie conceptualized the problem in 1889, "The man who dies leaving behind him millions of available wealth, which was his to administer during his life, will pass away 'unwept, unhonored, and unsung,' no matter to what uses he leaves the dross which he cannot take with him. Of such as these the public verdict will then be: 'The man who dies thus rich dies disgraced.'"

Underlying the Gospel of Wealth, a number of factors may have influenced philanthropists like Hershey and Carnegie to give away their fortunes, including a genuine desire to do something noble, possible feelings of guilt about their wealth in relation to the masses, the acclaim and respect of others paid to the philanthropists for their generosity, the promise of immortality associated with having one's name attached to their gifts (Carnegie Hall, the Hershey School, the Milton Hershey Medical Center, Carnegie Mellon University), and religious conviction. More often than not some combination of these factors played into their decisions. While Milton and Catherine Hershey always evidenced a deep concern for others, for instance, they only opened their school for orphans in 1909 after they discovered they could not have children. This is not to say that they would not have done so otherwise but to emphasize the myriad of influences that likely factored into their decision.

There was, of course, a flip side to the humanitarianism displayed by Hershey. Despite his great love and admiration for his wife—in fact he often credited her with the idea of opening the home and school—only white male boys were admitted until 1968. Female students were not admitted until 1976. This, of course, was consistent with the prevailing sentiments of the time. It does not diminish Hershey's humanitarianism. It simply demonstrates for students the importance of history in charting how social, economic, political, and cultural conditions have changed over time. It also reminds us of the importance of the individual in history and the idea that people can make a difference. As Dennis Denenberg and Lorraine Roscoe (2001) explain in their wonderful book *50 American Heroes Every Child Should Meet*, heroes are human beings who make mistakes and have limitations like everyone else. In studying their lives we may come to appreciate ways to enhance our own.

Cold Case #1868

> The greatest of all Western gunmen was John Wesley Hardin of Texas. In a seven-year period he killed more than 20 men—more than Billy the Kid or Jesse James, who surpassed him in notoriety. Hardin never killed for money and, although often a fugitive from justice, was not a criminal in the usual sense of the word. Rather, as a killer he was the product of his place and time. (Brown, 1970)

In my AP history classes, I sometimes added an extra layer to teach historiography. Unlike the previous cases in this chapter, the focus in this Cold Case is not on the unrevealed identity of an individual, but on a passage from a secondary text that requires students to enter into dialogue and debate with the historian about his or her interpretation of the individual's significance. One of my favorite such cases deals with the Texas outlaw John Wesley Hardin, described in the box above. Born in 1856, Hardin went on to become one of the more notorious gunslingers in the West. In a chapter devoted to Hardin in his useful document-based reader *American Violence*, historian Richard Maxwell Brown (1970) describes the feared Texan as "peerless," "not a criminal in the usual sense of the word," and "a product of his time and place" (p. 69). This edited quotation from Brown translated into a tantalizing scrap of evidence for my student detectives.

After sharing this evidence with my students, I asked them to consider a number of questions about the edited document, in other words, the content scene. They were

- How could Hardin kill 20 people and escape justice for so long?
- How could he have been "peerless," without equal, and yet remain largely unremembered, playing a second fiddle to the likes of Jesse James and Billy the Kid? (Incidentally, my students recognized both of them.)

- Could it have something to do with the time in which he lived and killed, or was it some other factor like his rationale for killing or even his victims?
- How, in light of such a murderous career, could Brown conclude that Hardin was "not a criminal in the usual sense of the word"?

Satisfied that my students had thoroughly interrogated the edited introduction by Brown, I handed them another piece of "evidence"—an excerpt from Hardin's autobiography recounting his first killing of a freedman named Madge in Texas in 1868 when he was just 15 years old.

In Hardin's Own Words

In the fall of 1868, I went down to my uncle's (Barnett Hardin) in Polk county, about four miles north of Livingstone. I was in the habit of making these trips, though I was then but 15 years old. This time they were making sugar and I took the trip to see them, carrying my pistol of course. I met a negro named Mage close to Moscow who had belonged to Judge Houlshousen, a brother to my Uncle Barnett Hardin's wife. I had a cousin named Barnett Jones who matched himself and me against this Moscow negro in a wrestling bout. The negro was a large, powerful man, and we were but two boys. Nevertheless we threw him down the first fall. He was not satisfied, so we threw him again, and this time scratched his face a little and made it bleed. Negro like he got mad and said he could whip me and would do it. Barnett and others standing around stopped us from fighting. This seemed to make Mage all the more angry. He said he would kill me, and went after his gun I went up to the house to get mine too, but Uncle Barnett got on to the game and made me stay in the house, while that negro went around cursing an abusing me saying "that he would kill me or die himself; that no white boy could draw his blood and live; that a bird never flew to high not to come to the ground." Uncle Barnett then took a hand and ordered Mage off the plantation.

FIGURE 2.4

Source: Wikipedia: Old West Gunfighters.

(Continued)

(Continued)

[Hardin came upon Mage the following day.] I stopped in the road and he came at me with his big stick. He struck me, and as he did it I pulled out a Colt's .44 six-shooter and told him to get back. By this time he had my horse by the bridle, but I shot him loose. He kept coming back, and every time he would start I would shoot again and again until I shot him down. I went to Uncle Clabe Houlshousen and brought him and another man back to where Mage was lying. Mage still showed fight and called me a liar. If it had not been for my uncle, I would have shot him again. Uncle Houlshousen gave me a $20 gold piece and told me to go home and tell father all about the big fight; that Mage was bound to die, and for me to look out for the Yankee soldiers who were all over the country at that time. Texas like other states, was then overrun with carpetbaggers and bureau agents who had the United States Army to back them up in their meanness. Mage shortly died in November, 1868. This was the first man I ever killed, and it nearly distracted my father and mother when I told them. All the courts were then conducted by bureau agents and renegades, who were the inveterate enemies of the South and administered a code of justice to suit every case that came before them and which invariably ended in gross injustice to Southern people, especially to those who still openly held on to the principles of the South. To be tried at that time for the killing of a Negro meant certain death at the hands of a court, backed by Northern bayonets; hence my father told me to keep in hiding until that good time when the Yankee bayonet should cease to govern. Thus, unwillingly, I became a fugitive, not from justice be it known, but from the injustice and misrule of the people who had subjugated the South. (Hardin, 1977, p. 12)

As we were going through Hardin's writing, I asked my students if Hardin's own words could help us answer some of our questions. At this point, several students began to hypothesize about Hardin's career, attributing it to the period of Reconstruction and the race of his victims. Others, however, were more cautious. "How do we know all of his victims were Black?" one girl asked. "I would like to read more of his autobiography," another girl contributed. "How do we know that he is being honest here?" asked one of the boys. When we were finished, I gave them Brown's complete introduction along with two other long pieces from Hardin's autobiography. I then asked them to evaluate Brown's overall assessment that as a killer Hardin was "a product of his time." If they agreed with Brown, they had to identify at least three reasons why and provide evidence from the sources to support their observations. If they disagreed, they also had to identify at least three reasons why and uncover evidence in the sources to support their position. In the end, we debated the merits of both positions in a class discussion.

The assignment itself was multilayered, asking students in the end to consider not only Brown's "interpretation" of Hardin as a "product of his time," but also to make and defend their own position as well. If you wish to use a shorter second piece of evidence about Hardin, consider the first paragraph from Gary L. Roberts's entry on Hardin in *Violence in America: An Encyclopedia* (1999). After introducing Hardin as the gunfighter with "the greatest claim to the title of 'man killer,'" Roberts observed:

> In a span of nine or ten years he killed at least twenty, perhaps as many as fifty men. And yet, he was never regarded as a psychopath. Indeed, despite his penchant for homicide, he was a good husband and father, a man of his word and a Christian. He was not a thief, and worked variously as a farmer, cowboy, gambler, saloonkeeper, logger, and schoolteacher. Many Texans saw Hardin as a hero in their struggle against Reconstruction and amidst the hostility against blacks. Nevertheless, although the violent climate of the times doubtless contributed to his lethal disposition, his killings do not appear to have been motivated by Reconstruction issues. Many were personal quarrels. (pp. 90–91)

This is a good example of how primary sources and historiography can be used to enhance your Cold Case files.

QUESTIONS FOR REVIEW AND REFLECTION

1. After reading this chapter, who are some of the major figures in United States history that you feel might be good candidates for CSI files? Take a few moments to jot down a few names of those you think would be the most exciting to you and your students.

2. Take a brief survey of your state content standards. Who are some of the people that you could build cold cases around? What resources would you need to do so? Take a few moments to reflect on ways to incorporate other content from your content standards by using CSI.

3. The story of the revival of Pepsi Cola through the medium of jingle advertising is not a novel one. Can you think of any other corporations, television programs, or political slogans (e.g., cigarette manufacturer Phillip Morris' "You've Come a Long Way Baby" campaign for its brand Virginia Slims in 1968, inspired by women's liberation; the theme song from the NBC television show *Friends*, "I'll Be There For You" by the Rembrandts, which became a hit song in the 1990s and the theme song for a decade; or George Herbert Walker Bush's mantra "Read my lips" from the election of 1988) that have transcended their original purpose to become part of the popular culture? Would any of these make good Cold Cases?

4. What are some historiographic controversies like the debate over Bacon's Rebellion that might make interesting Cold Case files? How might you incorporate the CSI approach with historiographical debates you are already teaching?

REFERENCES

African Pygmy's fate is still undecided. (1906, September 18). *The New York Times*, p. 1. Reprinted in Williams, Y. *A constant struggle: African-American history 1865–present* (pp. 294–306). Dubuque, IA: Kendall Hunt.

Bradford, P. V. and Blume, H. (1992). *Ota Benga: The Pygmy in the Zoo*. New York: St. Martin's Press.

Brown, R. M. (Ed.). (1970). *American violence* (pp. 69-70). Englewood Cliffs, NJ: Prentice Hall.

Bushman shares a cage with Bronx apes. (1906, September 9). *The New York Times*, p. 1. Reprinted in Williams, Y. *A constant struggle: African-American history 1865–present* (pp. 294–306). Dubuque, IA: Kendall Hunt.

Carnegie, A. (1889). Wealth. *North American Review*. (Reprinted in *The Annals of America: Vol. 11. 1884–1894* (pp. 222–226). Chicago: Encyclopedia Britannica.)

Denenberg, D. and Roscoe, L. (2001). *50 American heroes every kid should meet*. Brookfield, CT: Millbrook Press.

Davidson, J. W. & Lytle, M. H. (1982). *After the fact: The art of historical detection*. New York: Knopf Publishing Group.

Hanley, C. (2000). "Dissenters vow to fight over Japanese American monument." *Asian Week*. Retrieved March 20, 2008, from http://asianweek.com/2000_07_13/news2_japanesemonumntfight.html

Hardin, J. W. (1977). *The life of John Wesley Hardin as written by himself*. Norman, Oklahoma: University of Oklahoma Press.

Man and monkey show disapproved by clergy. (1906, September 10). *The New York Times*, p. 9. Reprinted in Williams, Y. *A constant struggle: African-American history 1865–present* (pp. 294–306). Dubuque, IA: Kendall Hunt.

Roberts, G. (1999). John Wesley Hardin. In R. Gottesman (Ed.), *Violence in America: An Encyclopedia*. New York: Charles Scribner's Sons.

Washburn, W. E. (1972). *The Governor and the rebel: A history of Bacon's Rebellion in Virginia*. New York: W. W. Norton. (Original work published 1957.)

Wertenbaker, T. J. (1965). *Torchbearer of the revolution: The story of Bacon's Rebellion and its leader*. Gloucester, MA: Peter Smith. (Original work published 1940.)

Wiggins, G. & McTighe, J. (1988). *Understanding by design*. Alexandria, VA: Association for Supervision and Curriculum Development.

Williams, Y. (2003). *A constant struggle: African-American history 1865–present* (pp. 294–306). Dubuque, IA: Kendall Hunt.

RESOURCES AND FURTHER READING

Davis, C. & Kovac, J. (2006). Confrontation at the locks: A protest of Japanese removal and incarceration during World War II. *Oregon Historical Quarterly, 107*, 486–509.

This short article on the removal of the Japanese is good for building teacher content knowledge.

Denenberg, D. and Roscoe, L. (2001). *50 American heroes every kid should meet*. Brookfield, CT: Millbrook Press.

Rich in content and beautifully written, this book also puts 50 possible Cold Case subjects right at your fingertips with all the information you need to craft your case.

Erdman, T. M. (1994). Hershey: Sweet smell of success. *American History Illustrated, 29(1)*, 64–69, 71.

This is a short student-friendly source on Milton Hershey.

Evans, R. W. (1988). Lessons from history: Teacher and student conceptions of the meaning of history. *Theory and Research in Social Education 16(3)*, 203–224.

This article examines the different ways that teachers and students conceptualize the meaning of history and calls for teachers to clearly converse with students about historical patterns, purpose, and relevance to stimulate student interest in history. This article was very useful in my early development of the CSI method.

Foster, S. J., & Yeager, E. A. (1993). The role of empathy in the development of historical understanding. *International Journal of Social Education, 13(1)*, 1–7.

The authors of this insightful article propose a four phase approach to helping students develop a sense of historical empathy that works well with the CSI method. They argue that appreciating empathy grows out of a process that begins with "the introduction of an historical event necessitating the analysis of human action, the understanding of historical context and chronology, the analysis of a variety of historical evidence and interpretations, and the construction of a narrative framework through which historical conclusions are reached" (p. 1).

Funderburg, A. C. (2001). *Sundae best: A history of soda fountains*. Bowling Green, OH: Bowling Green State University Popular Press.

This highly accessible book documents the history of some of the United States' biggest soft drinks makers. It is an excellent source on Caleb Bradham and Pepsi but also could be used to investigate the local history of other soft drink manufacturers like Atlanta born Coca-Cola.

Livesay, H. (1975). *Andrew Carnegie and the rise of big business*. Boston: Houghton Mifflin.

This is a good study of Andrew Carnegie that treats the steel magnate in relation to the rise of big business during the Gilded Age.

Martin, M. W. (1962). *Twelve full ounces*. New York: Holt, Rinehart and Winston.

This book provides a short history of the birth, near death, and rebirth of Pepsi Cola.

Masaoka, M. and Hosokawa, B. (1987). *They call me Moses Masaoka: An American saga*. New York: Morrow.

This is Mike Masaoka's very interesting autobiography. It is a must read for those interested in the struggle for civil rights waged by Asian Americans in twentieth-century America.

McGinty, B. (1982). John Wesley Hardin: Gentleman of guns. *American History Illustrated 17(4)*, 32–36.

This is another useful resource on John Wesley Hardin.

Rhodes, G. (1977). What happened to the Showers brothers? and other local mysteries: Bringing local history into the classroom. *New England Social Studies Bulletin, 34(2)*, 23–26.

This is a neat article exploring how to incorporate local history into your teaching through the use of local legends and mysteries.

Scott, C. (2001). Pygmy in the zoo: The story of Ota Benga. *Bronx County Historical Society Journal, 38(2)*, 84–95.

This short accessible article on the exhibition of Ota Benga is an ideal source for teachers looking to assign a longer reading than the newspaper accounts to their students.

Stamps, J. A. and Stamps, R. (Eds.). (2002). The letters of John Wesley Hardin. *Southwestern Historical Quarterly, 105*, 698–700.

This is a good resource for finding primary sources on John Wesley Hardin.

ON THE WEB

Many of the Web resources for Haunted History can also be used to identify subjects for potential CSI cases. Here are a few additional Web-based resources to get you started.

The Center for Teaching History with Technology. (n.d.). Retrieved March 20, 2008, from http://thwt.org/

This user-friendly site provides resources for history and social studies teachers including lesson plans, activities, and assessment items that integrate technology in the classroom. This is a great place to begin if you are looking for ways to incorporate technology such as Power Point presentations into your CSI and Haunted History projects.

Center for History and New Media: History Matters. (n.d.). Retrieved March 20, 2008, from http://historymatters.gmu.edu/

Designed primarily with the needs of high school and college teachers and students in mind, *History Matters* is nonetheless a useful tool for history teachers at all levels. The site serves as an access point to U.S. history on the Web resources, providing links to a variety of resources online.

Library of Congress. (n.d.). *Learning Page.* Retrieved March 20, 2008, from http://lcweb2 .10c.gov/ammem/ndlpedu/

With over 7 million historical documents, maps, photographs, audio recordings and films, you will find no shortage of materials here for creating exciting CSI and Haunted History files. The site also includes lesson plans searchable by topic, time, or theme. On the whole, this site is one of the best resources for teaching American history.

3

Historical Fingerprinting

Analyzing Primary and Secondary Sources

Being courier to the past is not enough. For better or worse, historians inescapably leave an imprint as they go about their business: asking interesting questions about apparently dull facts, seeing connections between subjects that had not seemed related before, shifting -and rearranging-evidence until it assumes a coherent pattern. The past is not history; only the raw material of it.

—James West Davidson and Mark Hamilton Lytle (1982)

"The wonderful and daunting thing about the young," historian James Axtell (2001) opined, "is that they live so thoroughly and energetically in the present with much more attention to the future than to the past" (p. 433). There is, however, a way to turn this seeming liability into a gateway into historical inquiry without pandering to current fads. Because students live in the present, they are often shocked to find the "historical roots" of their world in the world gone by. Thus, when teachers engage their students in Historical Fingerprinting of primary and secondary sources, they open up a world in which those in the past remain in dialogue with those in a more distant past, those in the present, and, through the student, those in the future.

If historical figures left "psychic" impressions that remained long after their time on earth, as we have uncovered with HOST Files, it seems reasonable, using historical forensics, that they might leave other evidence—physical evidence of their time here—as well. This could include everything from their writings, such as official documents and correspondence, to other kinds of sources included in the five typologies of primary sources.

1. Print documents

2. Electronic media

3. Folklore, folkways, and mythology

4. Fine arts and graphic arts

5. Built environments and artifacts (Danzer & Newman, 1991)

It also could include less tangible forms of evidence: traces of their thoughts, ideas, methods, techniques, approaches—in other words their intellectual fingerprints—scattered throughout time. By making their students junior forensics investigators, teachers can help students appreciate this aspect of historical research and inquiry through a method I call Historical Fingerprinting. The key to Historical Fingerprinting lies in the presentation of the "evidence" and in the use of the technique to get students to think critically about what they have found in the process of drawing conclusions. It also allows you, as the teacher, to model not just examining but interpreting the findings as you join the class in the search for evidence of those who have gone before and in search of the lasting impressions that those people have had on the present. Historical Fingerprinting might be described as the training wheels on the way to higher-order thinking about primary and secondary sources because it neatly encapsulates some of the basic *who, what, why, where,* and *how* questions with the more advanced questions that historians ask.

LEARNING TO THINK LIKE A HISTORIAN

Historical thinking, after all, does not develop naturally, or so Sam Wineburg proposed in his celebrated book *Historical Thinking and Other Unnatural Acts* (2001). On a mission to find out how historians process information, Wineburg discovered important differences between the way teachers, students, and professional historians read historical documents. Wineburg illustrates how the historian at work employs four important tools in exploring primary sources. They include what he calls the "sourcing heuristic," the "corroboration heuristic," contextualization, and comparative thinking. Each of these tools helps historians draw conclusions about the meaning, validity, and context of a primary source.

Historians' Four Tools (Wineburg, 2001)

1. The *sourcing heuristic* may be defined as the questions historians put to a document to establish its meaning and relevance. These include basic questions concerning the author's identity, the occasion, the intended audience, and the reason for producing the document. For history students, the old History Alive mnemonic of SOAP (source, occasion, audience and purpose) neatly approximates the sourcing heuristic. In engaging the source, occasion, audience, and purpose, students can easily understand the basic information about a document.

2. The *corroboration heuristic* is trickier. Wineburg explains that historians use the corroboration heuristic to substantiate, compare, and contrast information gleaned from a document with other primary sources with which they are familiar as well as with other historians' interpretations of the past. This is where we will be applying the concept of Historical Fingerprinting.

3. For Wineburg *contextualization* involves historians looking at the wider context or circumstances under which a primary source was produced. This can include everything from social, economic, and political conditions to language and fashion. These can provide import clues to what was going on locally and nationally and how that might have influenced the author of the document or artifact under consideration. Take a second look, for example, at historian Richard Maxwell Brown's (1970) introduction to John Wesley Hardin in Chapter 2. Later in his introduction (in a passage not reproduced in Chapter 2) Brown explains of Hardin, "He grew up in the violent region of central Texas and as a youth was ardently pro-Southern an anti-Negro. He fell into his death-dealing career not from any design but as a result of the racial, political, and family-feud tensions that converged upon him in the turbulent reconstruction era of Texas." (Brown, 1970, p. 69) In this passage Brown seeks to contextualize Hardin's life for his readers.

4. Lastly historians engage in *comparative thinking*; that is, they look to make comparisons between what was happening in the United States and other parts of the world when the source was produced in an effort to gain deeper insight and understanding about the source.

The use of Wineburg's four tools is what largely distinguishes professional historians from history teachers and advanced history students. For example, when students read a document like the Pure Food and Drug Act (PFDA) of 1906 , they likely will see it as an important effort to deal with unsanitary conditions in the nation's food producing industries shortly after the turn of the century. In the hands of the historian, the same document becomes a window into not only the reforms themselves, but also a laboratory to test the arguments of other historians on the nature of Progressive Reform itself.

Historians, for example, have long contested the origins and meaning of the Progressive Movement. Historian Richard Hofstadter (1955) argued that the movement grew out of the "status anxiety" of fading elites determined to reestablish their leadership and relevance in a rapidly changing society. Further developed by Joseph Gusfield (1963), this view of Progressivism was dominant until Robert Wiebe (1967) claimed to locate the origins of the movement in the aspirations of an emerging new middle class that sought to assert itself on the national stage.

Like a criminalist at a crime scene, the professional historian would not simply look at the PFDA's connection to the Progressive Movement but also attempt to corroborate the various interpretations of the same evidence offered by other historians. In so doing, the historian could be said to be "dusting for the fingerprints" of both Hofstadter and Gusfield's displaced elite and Wiebe's determined middle class reformers in the authors and signers of the bill, in an effort to establish which interpretation provides a more accurate portrait of the movement. Historians, for instance, would pore over the PFDA in search of clues supporting or contradicting one or both of these interpretations and, based on their reading of the evidence, offer their own. Wineburg explains that historians, after using the sourcing and corroboration heuristics, contextualize the information and engage in comparative thinking in an effort to tease out the larger significance of the document.

WHAT IS HISTORICAL FINGERPRINTING?

Getting students to perform the complex analysis described above might seem an overwhelming task, but Historical Fingerprinting can help. Like the corroborative heuristic, the science of fingerprinting depends on comparisons. In an effort to corroborate the evidence and convert primary sources, the raw material of history, into a cogent and accurate reflection of the past, the students have to first prep the document by "SOAPing" it to establish the basic information of source, occasion, audience, and purpose. Then they "fingerprint" it, looking for antecedent and modern connections, as well as its relationship to how others have sought to interpret the past. The reason why these two methods work well together is partly rooted in their real life functions. Use too much soap, and you may wash away valuable evidence in the form of fingerprints. Focus too narrowly on *who, what,* and *where,* and you forget that good historians, like good detectives, must also explain the *how* and *why,* if they wish to convince others of the thoroughness of their interpretation.

While there are other models, including an excellent worksheet produced by the Library of Congress and the National Archives, that one can use to approximate the corroborative heuristic, Historical Fingerprinting engages students at a level where the process is simplified. The teacher, therefore, can ease them into this type of higher-order

thinking with an exercise that is both useful and fun. This is a great way to introduce students to primary sources by
dressing up what can be a rather dry
exercise with a more compelling layer of
science and mystery.

FIGURE 3.1

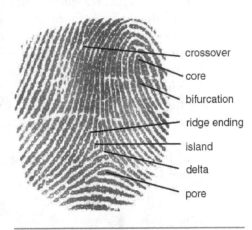

crossover

core

bifurcation

ridge ending

island

delta

pore

Source: International Biometric Group.

Although the main point of fingerprinting is to draw comparisons, each set
of fingerprints is unique. In fact the standard definition of a fingerprint is "a unique
characteristic, mark, or pattern that can be
used to identify somebody or something"
(Fingerprint, 2007). Even with sophisti-
cated computer programs that can now
search through thousands of prints in a
short period of time, the basic underpinnings of the analysis remain the same.
Computer programs compare seven identifiable characteristics of fingerprints; in Historical Fingerprinting, students look at four aspects: Island,
Core, Crossover, and Bifurcation (see Figure 3.1). This is how they are used.

Island

In fingerprinting Island is defined as a line-type, which stands alone
(that is, a line that does not touch another line-type and is wholly con-
tained in the pattern area of interest). In Historical Fingerprinting, Island
might best be described as the context for the primary source and its relation to its immediate historical circumstances. In other words, what makes
it unique or special? Time and place are important considerations here.
When and where a primary source was generated, as well as why and
how, tells us something important about the source that makes it unique
from all others.

Used in conjunction with SOAP, Island should therefore set the document in its proper historical context while addressing the basic questions
of *who, what, when, where,* and *why.* It engages the author of the source,
including his or her primary or intended audience as well as the occasion
and purpose of the document. For example, Abigail Adams's appeal for
the rights of women can easily be compared with other such appeals
across time, but the circumstances of her writings, as well as her position,
are what make them unique. Abigail Adams was writing during a specific
time when the social, political, and economic opportunities for women
were extremely limited. Her primary audience was her husband John.
Theirs was an intimate correspondence rather than a public communication. Students learn to appreciate how that might have shaped what she
wrote and why. Alexander Stephens, the Vice President of the Confederacy,

delivered his famous Cornerstone Speech to address a different set of circumstances, the secession of the Confederate states from the Union and the philosophical foundations of their new government. In it, he was careful to distinguish between earlier conflicts and the circumstances leading to the formation of the Confederacy. As he explained, "The new constitution has put at rest, forever, all the agitating questions relating to our peculiar institution—African slavery as it exists amongst us—the proper status of the negro in our form of civilization. This was the immediate cause of the late rupture and present revolution" (Alexander, 1998). In addressing Island questions, historical detectives should carefully weigh these SOAP and Island factors in establishing the context of the primary source under consideration.

Core

The Core of a fingerprint is the area situated within the innermost recurring ridge. Normally it is located in the middle of the fingerprint. In this sense it is the heart of the print. In Historical Fingerprinting, the Core likewise is the centerpiece or the heart of the document. It asks what the main point of the primary source is. It calls for students to read and thoroughly understand the document. For example, what are the three or four core issues raised by Abigail Adams in her correspondence with her husband regarding women and the revolution? Likewise, what were the key arguments advanced by her? As an additional tool for understanding the document's Core argument, teachers might consider having their students apply the ESP formula. Since, as noted in Chapter 1, content standards rely heavily on ESP, using this formula can provide yet another opportunity for students to see why these factors are so popular in the study of history and what value they have as an initial method of inquiry.

Crossover

In forensic science a crossover is defined as a short ridge that runs between two parallel ridges. It connects two independent ridges. In Historical Fingerprinting, the Crossover is the fun part. It allows students to access prior knowledge and invites them to make similar connections with things they have studied in the past. It also allows you, through modeling fingerprinting, to foreshadow things to come as well as revisit and review previous content. Crossover is the students' time machine. It reinforces the concept that historical actors are in dialogue with one another and allows students to practice the corroboration heuristic at a level consistent with their knowledge and ability. Getting students to make connections can be as simple as asking them to imagine dialogues between historical actors, both in the immediate historical moment and across time. What, for instance, would Abigail Adams say to Rosa Parks if they could have a conversation? More provocatively, what marital advice might Catherine the Great have offered Abigail Adams? You might also ask students to identify names or terms that they do not know and investigate why they were invoked in the primary source. Have your students consider any such terms as additional "suspects" in your CSI investigation (see Chapter 2), and encourage them to identify and fingerprint them as well. These can be really fun for students.

Crossover, therefore, is not what Kevin Kern and Kathren Brown (2001) describe as the superficial and false connections students sometimes make between great historical figures. Kern and Brown reference, as an example, the well-known coincidental comparisons between the assassinations of Abraham Lincoln and John F. Kennedy. Crossover is, in fact, comparative history at its best, connecting for instance the ideas of the Enlightenment in Europe to the American, French, and Haitian Revolutions or linking movements for national unification in the United States, Italy, and Germany. It can help students take that important first step away from simple regurgitation of the facts to true comparative thinking.

Bifurcation

In the science of fingerprinting, bifurcation refers to the point in a fingerprint where a ridge divides to form two ridges that continue past the point of division for a distance that is at least equal to the spacing between adjacent ridges at the point of the split. In law, bifurcation is a judge's ability to divide a trial into two parts to render a judgment on a set of legal issues without looking at all aspects. Civil cases are frequently bifurcated into separate liability and damages actions. For example, a divorce may be granted before issues of marital property, custody, and support are resolved.

In historical fingerprinting, bifurcation refers to the splitting of the main body of an argument into two parts. It can refer to a person who has historical relevance for two groups of people or movements. Sojourner Truth's "Ain't I a Woman?" speech, for example, can be read as an appeal both for the end of slavery and for women's rights. Consider Truth's words as reported by Frances Gage (Stanton, 1969, pp. 114–117). One of the reasons this makes a great historical fingerprinting exercise is that it is also a CSI "crime scene." Recently scholars have questioned the authenticity of the speech since Gage published the account in 1881 more than 30 years after the event. Think of the multilayered unit you could create with the document and the controversy utilizing historical fingerprinting, CSI, and SOAP.

Ain't I a Woman?

Well, children, where there is so much racket there must be something out of kilter. I think that 'twixt the negroes of the South and the women at the North, all talking about rights, the white men will be in a fix pretty soon. But what's all this here talking about?

That man over there says that women need to be helped into carriages, and lifted over ditches, and to have the best place everywhere. Nobody ever helps me into carriages, or over mud-puddles, or gives me any best place! And ain't I a woman? Look at me! Look at my arm! I have ploughed and planted, and gathered into barns, and no man could head me! And ain't I a woman? I could work as much and eat as much as a man—when I could get it—and bear the lash as well! And ain't I a woman? I have borne thirteen children, and seen most all sold off to slavery, and when I cried out with my mother's grief, none but Jesus heard me! And ain't I a woman?

Then they talk about this thing in the head; what's this they call it? [member of audience whispers, "intellect"] That's it, honey. What's that got to do with women's rights or negroes' rights? If my cup won't hold but a pint, and yours holds a quart, wouldn't you be mean not to let me have my little half measure full? (MacNeil, 2006)

Celebrated for doing something positive in one aspect of their lives and criticized for their actions in other aspects, individuals might also be bifurcated. President Lyndon Baines Johnson, for example, can be celebrated for the war on poverty and his movement on civil rights and yet challenged for the escalation of the war in Vietnam. Like branches that spring from the same vine, issues bifurcate as well. This also works with public policy. The idea of American isolationism has bifurcated over the years, reflecting the historical circumstances (Island) of the times when it has arisen. The same is true for immigration reform at various points in United States history, as well as for imperialism and territorial expansion. One could easily point to examples of bifurcation in social movements such as the women's rights movement or the civil rights movement.

Black Power

For many years historians saw the Black Power Movement as the evil twin that destroyed the cohesiveness and non-violent focus of the mainstream civil rights movement. Blamed for igniting civil disturbances and inspiring radical political movements, the Black Power Movement was interpreted as the unfortunate response of certain segments of the African American community to the slow pace of racial change in the late 1960s. The Black Power Movement was thus seen as branching off from the civil rights movement after Stokley Carmichael's call for Black Power in the summer of 1966. In his recent book, *Waiting 'Til the Midnight Hour: A Narrative History of Black Power in America*, historian Peniel Joseph (2006) argues that the civil rights movement and the Black Power Movement were actually parallel movements and that a wide diversity of opinion on the best course of action within both movements led to more radical splinters and branches. One could have, for example, militant advocates for civil rights who broke with the main body of the movement over issues such as armed self defense but who were not necessarily in favor of the same types of goals articulated by the proponents of Black Power, who in a more general sense accepted the need for armed self defense.

Like most of the strategies in this book, Historical Fingerprinting is a means to an end. It is designed to both simplify and demystify the historical process. It is also useful in helping students practice thinking like historians consistent with the goals articulated by local, state, and national history and social studies standards. The National Standards for History composed by the National Council for History in the Schools (1995), for instance, identified two types of standards: those that assess historical understanding and those that seek to develop historical thinking skills. The following are the five interconnected dimensions of historical thinking:

1. Chronological thinking

2. Historical comprehension

3. Historical analysis and interpretation

4. Historical research capabilities

5. Historical issues-analysis and decision-making

Historical Fingerprinting is tailor-made to achieve standards because it is always pushing students to look for important crossovers by respecting the other elements of historical inquiry.

CONSTRUCTING A HISTORICAL FINGERPRINTING KIT

In constructing a Historical Fingerprinting Kit teachers might want first to select a few primary sources including documents, photographs, and political cartoons. Some of the primary documents that can be used to introduce Historical Fingerprinting are listed below. While far from exhaustive, and only intended as a way to stimulate your thinking about how to apply Historical Fingerprinting in your own instruction, the documents presented here are ones that relate to persons or events that most often appear in the various state history and social studies standards. These include the American Revolution, the Civil War, and the struggles for civil rights and women's rights. They are also ones that in my experience yield the best Crossovers and Bifurcations.

Thomas Jefferson, the Declaration of Independence (1776)

Correspondence between Abigail Adams and John Adams (1776)

James Monroe, the Monroe Doctrine (1823)

David Walker's Appeal (1829)

Maria Stewart's Farewell Address (1833)

Declaration of Sentiments, Seneca Falls Conference (1848)

Sojourner Truth, "Ain't I a woman" speech (1851)

Abraham Lincoln, Cooper Union Address (1860)

Alexander Stephens, Cornerstone Speech (1861)

Abraham Lincoln, Gettysburg Address (1863)

Chief Joseph, "I will fight no more forever" surrender speech (1877)

Jane Addams, "The Subjective Necessity for Social Settlements" (1892)

John Marshall Harlan's dissent in *Plessey v. Ferguson* (1896)

Booker T. Washington, Atlanta Exposition Speech (1895)

Chinese Exclusion Act (1882)

Josiah Strong, *Our Country* (1885)

Theodore Roosevelt, Roosevelt Corollary (1905)

Woodrow Wilson, Fourteen Points Address (1918)

Franklin Roosevelt, Four Freedoms Address (1941)

George Kennan, *American Diplomacy* (1951)

Rachel Carson, *Silent Spring* (1962)

Martin Luther King Jr., "I have a dream" speech (1963)

The Black Panther Ten Point Program (1966)

Jeane Kirkpatrick, "Blame America First" speech to the Republican National Convention (1984)

Fingerprinting a Document

1. Hand out the document. As a general rule try to select documents with clear connections to content you have covered or will cover later. For example if you know that you want to do a fingerprinting exercise on Martin Luther King Jr. later in the year, be sure to cover other sources like Abigail Adams' correspondence with John Adams or Henry David Thoreau's "Civil Disobedience" (1849) that have clear connections to King.

2. SOAP the document, that is, have your students identify the source, occasion, audience, and purpose of the document.

3. Hand out a worksheet that identifies the four key elements of historical fingerprinting. Do the same thing on the chalk board. Assign a scribe or scribes to keep track of the ideas expressed for each. Either reading the document aloud as a class or assigning the students to read quietly to themselves, have the students look to uncover the Island and Core of the document. If you are doing the exercise as a class ask leading questions to help stimulate discussion. For example, after identifying the date of the document ask your students, "What can we possibly learn about the Core and Island of the document from the date?"

4. After your students have identified elements of the document related to the Island and Core, ask them to consider if there is any Crossover with content that you have covered in the past or if the issues covered in the document remind them of anything else they might have heard about or read regarding the ideas set forth. If you were reading a document, or viewing an image, that borrows from or engages ideas similar to a document, cartoon, or photograph you have examined before, ask broad questions to help students make those connections, such as "Where have we seen this before?" For example, if you are discussing calls for American isolation during the First World War, look to help students make connections between this isolationist strain and other content you have likely covered, including John Winthrop's "City upon a Hill" (1630), Washington's Farewell Address (1796), and the Monroe Doctrine (1823). In a general sense all of these documents expressed the need for Americans (in Winthrop's case, the colonists) to remain detached from European distresses.

5. After you have established your Crossovers, ask the students to look for Bifurcations. Using the previous example, how had the arguments in favor of isolationism or noninvolvement in European conflicts change over time, appealing to and being championed by a wide variety of persons and groups?

6. When you have all of the information up on the board, debrief the students by engaging them in discussion about the roots or fingerprints they found related to the document.

By using Historical Fingerprinting, teachers can select more obscure documents and still connect the content to testable items through the Crossover, relating them back to documents that appear in the content standards.

Historical Fingerprinting can help guide students through the documents, providing them with a clear focus and standard set of questions to help them get to the heart of the document and tease out its broader implications. Because Historical Fingerprinting neatly encapsulates the main questions posed by historians to any documents, it can become an indispensable tool for students in the pursuit of their own knowledge and understanding.

A SAMPLING OF HISTORICAL FINGERPRINTING AT WORK

Using Historical Fingerprinting in conjunction with other strategies presented in this book such as CSI and Haunted History opens up a world of teaching possibilities. With CSI, students dissect the documents in search of a plausible explanation of the past, based on available evidence and intended to be true. The use of CSI and Historical Fingerprinting compels them to make judgments about the facts and evidence. Here are some examples of the use of Historical Fingerprinting.

Fingerprinting the Declaration of Independence

If your students examine the Declaration of Independence for fingerprints and turn up evidence of the Enlightenment, guide them to look for other evidence to corroborate the influence of the Enlightenment on the mindset of the colonists on the eve of the rupture with Great Britain.

When discussing the Declaration of Independence, it is important to note that Thomas Jefferson and the Founding Fathers were in dialogue with other thinkers of the Enlightenment. In outlining their grievances to King George III, they addressed their protest to a wider world. As Jefferson wrote,

> When, in the course of human events, it becomes necessary for one people to dissolve the political bonds which have connected them with another, and to assume among the powers of the earth, the separate and equal station to which the laws of nature and of nature's God entitle them, a decent respect to the opinions of mankind requires that they should declare the causes which impel them to the separation.

Jefferson's reference to "a decent respect for the opinions of mankind" placed him and the other Founders on a world stage in dialogue with other thinkers on the nature of government and its obligations to its citizenry.

Women's Rights

Even as the Founders made their Core argument clear in voicing their problems with the British monarchy, their "subordinates," inspired by the revolutionaries' example, sought to address the inequality they experienced in their own relationships. As John Adams explained in a letter dated April 14, 1776, "We have been told that our struggle has loosened the bonds of government everywhere; that children and apprentices were disobedient; that schools and colleges were grown turbulent; that Indians slighted their guardians, and negroes grew insolent to their masters." He was writing in response to a letter from his wife, Abigail, whose own demand that women too be counted caught him by surprise. "Your letter," he confessed, "was the first intimation that another tribe, more numerous and powerful than all the rest, were grown discontented." Abigail Adams, as much a child of the Enlightenment as Jefferson and Adams, raised the issue squarely with her husband in March of 1776. "I long to hear that you have declared an independency," She wrote, "And, by the way, in the new code of laws which I suppose it will be necessary for you to make, I desire you would remember the ladies and be more generous and favorable to them than your ancestors." Her interests were by no means limited to domestic harmony. Instead, she demanded the same freedom and liberty for women as claimed by the founders.

"Do not put such unlimited power into the hands of the husbands," she warned. "Remember, all men would be tyrants if they could. If particular care and attention is not paid to the ladies, we are determined to foment a rebellion, and will not hold ourselves bound by any laws in which we have no voice or representation." This was one of the first and most powerful examples of the language of the Declaration being used to attack inequalities and injustices within what would soon become the United States of America. It would certainly not be the last.

Alaskan Statehood

Throughout United States history, there are hundreds of significant examples (Crossovers and Bifurcation) of persons using the Declaration to demand equality, from the abolitionist movement to the women's movement to the demands by the District of Columbia, Puerto Rico, and Alaska for statehood. Note the language of Alaskan Senator Ernest Gruening (1967) in his celebrated appeal for statehood etitled, "Let Us Now End American Colonialism." Delivered on April 11, 1955, at the Alaska Constitutional Convention, Gruening began, "We meet to validate the most basic of American principles, the principle of 'government by consent of the governed." He continued by pointing out that argument for Alaskan statehood could be seen as in line with the ideas expressed in the Declaration of Independence.

Let Us Now End American Colonialism

America does not, alas, practice what it preaches, as long as it retains Alaska in colonial vassalage.

Is there any doubt that Alaska is a colony? Is there any question that in its maintenance of Alaska as a territory against the expressed will of its inhabitants, and subject to the accompanying political and economic disadvantages, the United States has been and is guilty of colonialism? . . . Let us recall the first item of grievance in the Declaration of Independence: 'He has refused assent to laws, the most wholesome and necessary for the public good.' 'He,' of course, was King George the Third. Put in his place, in place of the 'he,' his contemporary equivalent, our ruler, the federal government. Has it, or has it not, 'refused assent to laws most wholesome and necessary for the public good'?

For our nation was born of revolt against colonialism. Our charters of liberty—the Declaration of Independence and the Constitution—embody America's opposition to colonialism and to colonialism's inevitable abuses. It is therefore natural and proper that American leadership should set its face against the absenteeism, the discriminations and the oppressions of colonialism. It is natural and proper that American leadership should lend such aid and comfort as it may to other peoples striving for self-determination and for that universally applicable tenet of American faith—government by consent of the governed. Indeed, as we shall see, we are pledged to do this by recent treaty commitments.

Source: Ernest Gruening, "Let Us Now End American Colonialism," first delivered at the Alaska Constitutional Convention on April 11, 1955. Excerpted from Gruening (1967); also available online at the University of Alaska's Web site on the quest for statehood at http://www.alaska .edu/creatingalaska/convention/speeches/gruening.xml.

This strategy of asking Americans to live up to the ideals so eloquently expressed in the Declaration and affirmed in theory but denied in practice has been the source of bitter contention in United States history.

Dred Scott Decision

In the Dred Scott decision, Justice Roger B. Taney addressed the issue of inequality squarely. At the same time in dialogue with the Founders and with the abolitionists who used their words to rail against slavery, Taney sought to explain the seeming contradiction in the Founders' words and actions. The framers of the Declaration of Independence, argued the Chief Justice, were men of honor; therefore, when they continued to hold Africans in bondage while proclaiming universal human rights, they clearly could not have intended to include those of African descent among their vision of the people, for that would have made them hypocrites rather than principled men. As Taney explained, "They perfectly understood the meaning of the language they used, and how it would be understood by others; and they knew that it would not in any part of the civilized world be supposed to embrace the negro race, which, by common consent, had been excluded from civilized Governments and the family of nations, and

doomed to slavery." "They spoke and acted according to the then established doctrines and principles, and in the ordinary language of the day,"
Taney continued, "and no one misunderstood them." "The unhappy black
race," he concluded, "were separated from the white by indelible marks
and laws long before established, and were never thought of or spoken of
except as property, and when the claims of the owner or the profit of the
trader were supposed to need protection" (Dred Scott v. Sanford, 1856).

Engaging the Declaration

As we have seen, the debate over the meaning of the Declaration was
not limited to the question of slavery but would later encompass the quest
for expanded civil rights in the United States. In her answer to her
husband on May 7, 1776, Abigail Adams foreshadowed the course of that
later movement. "But you must remember," she warned, "that arbitrary
power is like most other things which are very hard, very liable to be bro-
ken; and, notwithstanding all your wise laws and maxims, we have it in
our power, not only to free ourselves, but to subdue our masters, and without violence, throw both your natural and legal authority at our feet."

The nonviolent civil rights movement led by the Reverend Dr. Martin
Luther King Jr. accomplished what Abigail Adams proposed. One cannot
escape the wonderful symbolism of Rosa Parks, the NAACP activist
whose refusal to give up her seat helped spark the Montgomery Bus
Boycott in the aftermath of the *Brown v. the Board of Education* decision,
which had itself directly challenged Justice Taney's interpretation of the
Declaration, as the very embodiment of Abigail Adam's words. What all of
these individuals have in common is their engagement of the Declaration
and then the Constitution with regard to freedom and equality in the
Republic—an understanding that your students can come to through the
use of methods like Historical Fingerprinting, which asks them to make
these types of connections. While the students' connections will be general
at first, as in the model I have presented here, over time you can expect
them to become quite comfortable looking for connections, especially if
you guide them to comparative thinking and analysis.

It is ultimately these connections or Crossovers that we would like our
students to be able to make in the course of reading about and interpreting the past. Historical Fingerprinting of primary sources can help move
them in that direction.

Fingerprinting the Preamble to the United States Constitution

While any historical primary source can be examined for fingerprints,
teachers should, at least initially, select documents in which Crossovers
are more readily apparent. One way to do this is to begin the process at
the beginning of the year with a simple technique using the Preamble to the
Constitution. I often tell my students on the first day of class that over the

course of the semester we will inquire about changes over time in the meaning and language of the Preamble. Take, for example, the words: "We the People." From the perspective of Island, "We the People" meant those white, property-owning males who gathered at the Constitutional Convention to restructure the fledgling government under the Articles of Confederation. The Core of their argument was straightforward: in the new order of things, governments derived their power from the consent of the governed. Over time, the question of who are "the people" shifted to accommodate the economic, social, cultural, and political growth and development of the young republic. The ever-expanding redefinition of citizenship, from the expansion of the voting populace under Andrew Jackson; to the inclusion of African American and naturalized immigrant males with the ratification of the 15th Amendment in 1870; to the 19th Amendment in 1920, which finally recognized women as citizens, provides fertile ground for Crossover connections. Equally important, the demands of various groups for citizenship and questions concerning immigration—from the Alien Act to the Chinese Exclusion Act, and from the internment of Japanese American citizens during the Second World War to debates over citizenship and immigration today— invite the kind of Crossover connections and critical thinking history and social studies demand.

Fingerprinting Political Cartoons

Here is an example of the application of Historical Fingerprinting using political cartoons.

Getting "Nasty"

Many teachers use political cartoons, and because Thomas Nast's career covers such a broad period—the Gilded Age and the Progressive Era—his cartoons are perhaps the most used of all. Historical Fingerprinting encourages students to interrogate Nast as much as his art. In their hunt to uncover other fingerprints, art, or artifacts that might better illuminate Nast's viewpoint on foreign immigration, the students will be pursuing leads much in the same way historians do.

Consider the political cartoon from Thomas Nast shown in Figure 3.2 concerning Chinese immigration in the decades after the Civil War. This cartoon is correlated with California's eighth-grade social studies standards as an example of how to correlate your unit with your state standards. Under California standard 8.12, "Students analyze the transformation of the American economy and the changing social and political conditions in the United States in response to the Industrial Revolution," point 7 reads:

Identify the new sources of large-scale immigration and the contributions of immigrants to the building of cities and the economy;

FIGURE 3.2   "Let the Chinese Embrace Civilization and They May Stay"

LET THE CHINESE EMBRACE CIVILIZATION, AND THEY MAY STAY.

Source: Harper's Weekly, November 13, 1880. Provided courtesy of HarpWest, LLC.

explain the ways in which new social and economic patterns encouraged assimilation of newcomers into the mainstream amidst growing cultural diversity; and discuss the new wave of nativism (California State Board of Education, n.d.).

Instead of having students simply identify the racial implications of the cartoon, consider having them identify and discuss the social, economic, political, and cultural overtones of that prejudice using Historical Fingerprinting. Be sure to reflect on Bifurcation. How is Nast's portrayal of the Chinese a significant departure from some of the more sympathetic images of minorities he produced in the immediate aftermath of the Civil War? What led him to depict racial and ethnic minorities as compromising the strength of the nation?

FIGURE 3.3   "A Truthful Protest Sign"

A Truthful Protest Sign

Source: Courtesy of Conservative News Service.

Recognizing Reality

At first glance, with its anti-war protesters and peace sign wearing centerpiece, this cartoon might be mistaken for something from the 1960s. Its origin is more recent, however, as the short haircut, baggy pants and the main protest sign's reference to "ex-hippie professor" portray. This is a good example of the Crossovers and Bifurcation that students can uncover using historical fingerprinting. As the visual clues and words suggest, the cartoonist blames the lack of a more vigorous anti-war effort against the Iraq conflict, similar to what the nation experienced in the 1960's, on today's "spoiled" and "self-indulgent" youth.

The cartoonist's point would be lost, however, without an understanding of the 1960s counterculture and the antiwar rallies that were so much a part of it. The artist also subtly opens up an opportunity to compare not only protests against the wars but also the Vietnam and Iraq wars themselves. It makes for a nice comparison of youth culture over time. It would be interesting to discuss some of the cartoonist's assessment of today's youth. As a final layer, consider having students compare the artist's assessment of today's youth with assessments of other generations. Journalist Tom Brokaw (2001), for example, has called the women and men who came of age during the Great Depression, fought the Second World War, and helped to build Modern America "The Greatest Generation." According to the cartoonist, how does this generation compare?

Dusting Secondary Sources

In the science of forensics, investigators make their case by piecing together the tiny scraps of evidence to explain what happened. Even with eyewitness testimony or a confession, forensic investigators must follow the evidence trail, no matter how minute, to corroborate the facts. In addition to primary sources, Historical Fingerprinting can be applied to the work of historians, who may be limited in their reconstruction of the past with partial or inadequate evidence. History, after all, is a patterned coherent account of the past, based on available evidence and intended to be true. A paucity of evidence or the inability to uncover corroborating evidence often influences judgments about the past.

The language associated with the science of fingerprinting is great for incorporating historiography into your students' investigations. For example, latent prints are fingerprints that are present but invisible to the naked eye. They can only become visible when dusted with chalk or other powders, or when viewed under the light of a laser. Sometimes the Core, Crossover, and/or Bifurcation of a document will not be readily apparent, so the student will need the tools of the historian to dust for the latent prints. This is a novel way to instruct students in the historian's use of interpretive frameworks, where the historian is purposely using a kind of interpretive laser to illuminate and reconcile the past with certain larger themes. Charles Beard's *Economic Interpretation of the Constitution* (1935/2001) immediately comes to mind. Like many of his earlier works, including *The Rise of American Civilization* (1927), it placed economics at the heart of the historical dialectic. Along with the concept of a "usable past" and "history from below," Beard's books illustrate how broader considerations or themes sometimes condition historians' questions.

From the National Center for History in the Schools

Historical understanding also requires that students thoughtfully read the historical narratives created by others. Well-written historical narratives are interpretative, revealing and explaining connections, change, and consequences. They are also analytical, combining lively storytelling and biography with conceptual analysis drawn from all relevant disciplines. Such narratives promote essential skills in historical thinking.

Reading such narratives requires that students analyze the assumptions—stated and unstated—from which the narrative was constructed and assess the strength of the evidence presented. It requires that students consider the significance of what the author included as well as chose to omit—the absence, for example, of the voices and experiences of other men and women who were also an important part of the history

(Continued)

(Continued)

of their time. Also, it requires that students examine the interpretative nature of history, comparing, for example, alternative historical narratives written by historians who have given different weight to the political, economic, social, and/or technological causes of events and who have developed competing interpretations of the significance of those events.

Source: National Standards for United States History and World History. "Chapter 2: Standards in Historical Thinking." (1995). The History Teacher, Vol. 28, No. 3, Exploring the National Standards for United States History and World History. pp. 315–334.

In other words, students need to fingerprint the authors of historical works to appreciate the source and force of their arguments. Students should be directed to look for the four elements of Historical Fingerprinting that correspond with the broader ideas identified by the National Center for History in the Schools. They should begin, for example, by asking what the Core of the authors' argument is. Put a different way, what is the main idea she or he is attempting to convey? Part of this process is assessing the overall strength of the author's thesis with regard to sources, voice, and omissions. Interrogating secondary sources also involves looking for Crossovers by comparing similar and alternative historical narratives. If your students used fingerprinting, for example, they could not only evaluate Charles Beard's argument with regard to alternative explanations offered by Gordon Wood in *The Creation of the American Republic, 1776–1787* (1969) and others, but also explore how class and economic interest shapes the historical process. This would also be applicable in comparing Beard's argument and conclusion with other historians who have emphasized class such as Leonard Richards in his book on anti-abolitionist mobs, *Gentleman of Property and Standing* (1970), and Richard Hofstadter (1955). In evaluating secondary sources, Island would come before Core, in the sense that it sets the context for what the author has written.

In the opening to every volume of the Harlan Davidson American History series, John Hope Franklin and Abraham Eisenstadt (Altschuler, 1982) write, "Every generation writes its own history for it tends to see the past in the foreshortened perspective of its own experience" (p. 1). In other words, our understanding of the past is influenced by the present and looks toward the future. As Franklin and Eisenstadt advise patrons of the series, "The practical aim of our historiography is to give us a more informed sense of where we are going by helping us to understand the road we took in getting where we are." In exploring secondary sources, Bifurcation, again, looks for the splitting of arguments into two or more parts. It examines how the works of certain historians have fueled the growth of interpretative schools of historiography and how these schools have led to subfields in history. While this line of inquiry would be most fruitful for advanced placement history students, middle school teachers can artificially introduce Bifurcation by selecting secondary sources that make clear references to other works.

QUESTIONS FOR REVIEW AND REFLECTION

1. This chapter presents a number of ways to incorporate Historical Fingerprinting into your instruction. What methods appeal to you most? Why? How might you implement them in your instruction?

2. This chapter discusses the use of Historical Fingerprinting with the other strategies in this book. How might you use Historical Fingerprinting with the other methods presented here? How about more traditional methods and strategies that you are currently using?

3. Review your state content standards. Do you see documents or themes that may lend themselves well to review by the process of Historical Fingerprinting? How might you adapt the Historical Fingerprinting exercise to meet your particular needs in this regard? How might you use fingerprinting to get students to make connections to content you have already covered?

REFERENCES

Alexander H. Stephens (1812–1883), Cornerstone Address, March 21, 1861. (1998). In Halsall, P. *Internet Modern History Sourcebook.* Retrieved March 20, 2008, from http://www.fordham.edu/halsall/mod/1861stephens.html

Altschuler, G. C. (1982). *Race, ethnicity, and class in American social thought 1865–1919.* Arlington Heights, IL: Harlan Davidson.

Axtell, J. (2001). The Pleasures of teaching. *The History Teacher, 34,* 433–446.

Beard, C. (1927). *The rise of American civilization.* (Vols. 1–2). New York: The Macmillan Company.

Beard, C. (2001). *An economic interpretation of the Constitution of the United States.* Union, NJ: Lawbook Exchange. (Original work published 1935.)

Brokaw, T. (2001). *The Greatest Generation.* New York: Dell Publishing.

Brown, R. M. (Ed.). (1970). *American violence* (pp. 69–70.). Englewood Cliffs, NJ: Prentice Hall.

California State Board of Education. (n.d.). *Grade Eight History–Social Science Content Standards.* Retrieved March 20, 2008, from http://www.cde.ca.gov/be/st/ss/hstgrade8.asp

Davidson, J.W. & Lytle, M.H. (1982). *After the fact: The art of historical detection.* New York: Knopf Publishing Group.

Danzer, G.A. & Newman, M. (1991). *Tuning in: Primary sources in the teaching of history.* Chicago: The World History Project.

Dred Scott v. Sandford, 60 U.S. 393 (1857). Retrieved March 24, 2008, from http://www.oyez.org/cases/1851–1900/1856/1856_0/

Fingerprint. (2007). In Microsoft Corporation, *Encarta world English dictionary.* Retrieved June 10, 2008, from http://encarta.msn.com/dictionary_1861611563/fingerprint.html

Gruening, E. (1967). *The Battle For Alaska Statehood.* Fairbanks: University of Alaska Press.

Gusfield, J. (1963). *Symbolic crusade; status politics and the American temperance movement.* Urbana: University of Illinois Press.

Hofstadter, R. (1955). *The age of reform; from Bryan to F. D. R.* New York: Knopf.

Joseph, P. (2006).*Waiting 'til the midnight hour: A narrative history of Black power in America.* New York: Henry Holt.

Kern, K. & Brown, K. (2001). Using *The list of creepy coincidences* as an educational opportunity [Electronic version]. *The History Teacher, 34,* 531–536.

MacNeil, R. (2006). *Malaspina great books.* Retrieved March 20, 2008, from http://www .malaspina.org/truths.htm

National Council for History in the Schools. (1995). Chapter 2: Standards in historical thinking. *The History Teacher, 28(3),* pp. 315–334.

Richards, L. *Gentlemen of property and standing: Anti-abolition mobs in Jacksonian America.* New York: Oxford University Press.

Stanton, E. C., Anthony, S. B., & Gage, M. J. (Eds.). (1881/1969). *History of Woman Suffrage.* New York: Arno Press.

Wineburg, Sam. (2001). *Historical thinking and other unnatural acts: Charting the future of teaching the past.* Philadelphia: Temple University Press.

Wiebe, R. (1967). *The search for order, 1877–1920.* New York: Hill and Wang.

Wood, G. (1969). *The creation of the American Republic, 1776–1787.* Chapel Hill: University of North Carolina Press.

RESOURCES AND FURTHER READING

Berkin, C. (2005). *Revolutionary mothers: Women in the struggle for America's independence.* New York: Knopf.

Carol Berkin's riveting study of the role of women in the American Revolution is a must read for its interesting view of the often overlooked contribution of women to this important chapter in American history.

Cullen, J. P. (1968). "Bacon's Rebellion." *American History Illustrated, 3,* 44–48.

A short accessible piece on Bacon's Rebellion for students, this article is also good for building teacher background knowledge of this episode in colonial American history.

Danzer, G. and Newman, M. (1991). *Tuning in: Primary sources in the teaching of history.* Chicago: The World History Project.

This is a wonderful resource on using primary sources in the classroom.

Drake, F. and Brown, S. (2003). "A systematic approach to improve students' historical thinking." *The History Teacher, 36,* 465–489.

This is an excellent article that outlines methods of teaching historical thinking.

Fournier, J. E., & Wineburg, S. S. (1997). "Picturing the past: Gender differences in the depiction of historical figures." *American Journal of Education, 105,* 160–185.

This very interesting study provides much food for thought in terms of the way we present issues relative to gender in the classroom. Based on students' overly male pictorial representations of history, among its findings is the real need for teachers to find a consistent means of discussing gender and the role of women more directly in our curriculum.

Keller, R. (1994). *Patriotism and the female sex: Abigail Adams and the American Revolution.* Brooklyn, NY: Carlson.

An interesting book on Abigail Adams during the American Revolution, this is a good starting place if you are looking to build background knowledge on Abigail.

Musbach, J. W. (2001) "Using primary sources in the secondary classroom." *OAH Magazine of History, Fall*, 30–32.

Musbach proposes five rules teachers should follow when using primary sources in the classroom. These include (1) making sure the sources are age appropriate; (2) that they are readable and accessible; (3) that there is sufficient background content to assist students in decoding; (4) that students work in small groups of two or three; and (5) that teachers should indicate a clear purpose and motivation to engage students in reading the documents. Historical Fingerprinting can be used in conjunction with much of what she discusses in this useful article.

Spencer, D. R. (1998). "Bringing down giants: Thomas Nast, John Wilson Bengough and the maturing of political cartooning." *American Journalism, 15,* 61–88.

This is a good source on the evolution of political cartoons and two of the cartoonists who helped transform them into a potent source of political commentary.

Stearns, P. N; Seixas, P.; and Wineburg, S. (Eds.). (2000). *Knowing, teaching, and learning history.* New York: New York University Press.

This outstanding collection of essays on teaching and learning history should be required reading for all teachers. Full of fresh insights and new perspectives on all aspects of historical thinking and instruction this book will definitely stimulate your thinking about new ways to approach classroom instruction and your own passion for history.

Wineburg, S. (2003). "Crazy for History." *Journal of American History, 90(4)*, 1401–1414.

This is a rich and provocative article by one of the leading minds in history education, who again makes the case for looking at new ways to invigorate history teaching. Wineburg's treatment of the three questions at the core of the continued debate over history instruction, including, what is the essence of historical understanding, how can historical interpretation and analysis be taught, and what is the role of instruction in improving students' ability to think, provides much to think about. Definitely add this to your reading list as you consider applying new methods like Historical Fingerprinting.

ON THE WEB

There are abundant resources for primary sources on the Web. In keeping with the structure of this book I am recommending the three that I think will be most useful to use as you apply the teaching methods presented here.

Teaching with documents: From the National Archives and Record Administration. (n.d.). Retrieved March 20, 2008, from http://www.archives.gov/education/lessons/

This is one of the most extensive primary source collections on the Web. Drawn largely from the National Archives' massive holdings, the site also includes teacher lesson plans correlated with the national standards in history and civics and government as well as an outstanding set of document analysis sheets ready for use in your classroom. The site's eight document analysis worksheets (covering everything from written documents to movies and sound recordings) all complement Historical Fingerprinting, making this an ideal site to begin thinking about Fingerprinting exercises with primary sources.

The Avalon project at Yale Law School: Documents in law, history and diplomacy. (1996–2007). Retrieved March 20, 2008, from http://www.yale.edu/lawweb/avalon/20th.htm

With full text copies of some of the most important documents in both United States and World History, this is by far my favorite resource for primary sources on the Web. One of the unique features of this site, especially for teachers looking to use Historical

Fingerprinting, are the in text links within many of the documents that identify and take the reader to the supporting documents quoted or referred to in the text. This is, of course, ideal for use with Historical Fingerprinting. Thus, while the focus of the documents is limited mostly to constitutional, legal and diplomatic history there is still a lot of material to draw from.

The Gilder Lehrman Institute of American History. (n.d.). Retrieved March 20, 2008, from http://www.gilderlehrman.org/collection/documents.html

With featured documents every two weeks, the Gilder Lehrman institute is another outstanding resource for finding primary sources. Equipped with a fairly good search engine, the site has much to offer in terms of relative ease of use and breadth and scope of the documents included.

4

The Intersection

Historical Accident Reconstruction

Citizenship has a moral agency in which the common good shares a stage with individualism. History plays a most significant role because of its power to create images and models of the actions taken by individuals and collectives to grapple with issues in the past.

—Fred Drake and Lynn Nelson (2004)

One of the more challenging concepts related to the study of history to communicate to students is the idea of agency. Agency is the idea that the people we study have made choices and that their actions have real significance. It explores the ways in which people have responded to social, economic, and political injustice and oppression and how their decisions to challenge, ignore, or acquiesce to the same have influenced not only the past but also the present.

This is not only limited to human action. Historians have long pondered the impact of geography on history. In recent years, a number of historians have pushed to recognize agency in nature. As historian Richard C. Foltz (2003) observed, nature has its own way of influencing the course of history. Certainly Hurricane Katrina, which struck the city of New Orleans with devastating force in 2005, reminds us of this important fact.

One important difference distinguishes natural occurrences from human agency, and that is that human agency is the product of conscious choices. Sorting out what went wrong as a result of any disruptive event involves a form of accident reconstruction, where teams of experts seek to piece together the answers to three essential questions:

1. What happened?
2. Why did it happen?
3. How can we prevent it from happening again?

If these questions sound familiar, it is because we have seen them before. Following yet another round of urban rioting in the summer of 1967, President Lyndon B. Johnson commissioned the National Advisory Commission on Civil Disorders, to become known as the Kerner Commission, and charged it with answering the same set of questions (National Advisory Commission on Civil Disorders, 1968).

This simple set of directives in many ways parallels our work as history and social studies educators. According to the National Council for the Social Studies, "Social studies educators teach students the content knowledge, intellectual skills, and civic values necessary for fulfilling the duties of citizenship in a participatory democracy" (National Council for the Social Studies, n.d.). In other words, a large part of what we do is related to what the Kerner Commission did. We try to make sense of the past while imparting a sense of civic responsibility.

One way to get students to understand these important historical processes is with a teaching strategy called Historical Accident Reconstruction, or simply the Intersection. It involves having students uncover the choices historical actors have made that resulted in important changes, from sweeping social reforms, to innovations in science and technology, to changes in the environment and responses to war and natural disasters that continue to impact our society.

WHAT IS THE INTERSECTION?

I first heard the concept of the Intersection articulated by Dr. Joseph Reidy while I was a graduate student at Howard University. He was explaining Reconstruction to a group of undergraduate history majors. It was the first day of class, and he offered a broad conceptualization of the problems posed by the end of the Civil War including what the status of those states that had seceded from the Union would be and the tensions over what to do with four million former slaves.

"Imagine that you have just pulled up to a busy four-stop intersection," he explained to the class, "and suddenly all the lights have gone out in the city. There is no way to determine who arrived at the intersection first, and there are no police or authorities around to appeal to for assistance." He continued, "The cars begin to stack up behind you. You can see the other cars waiting to enter the intersection across from you and to your left and right. What do you do? Do you remain at the downed stoplight and wait for the power to be restored, or do you move into the intersection?" He used this scenario to demonstrate the concept of historical agency—the idea that people make choices and that their actions have consequences that can change the course of history.

The Intersection as Accident Reconstruction

I immediately saw the value of the concept of the Intersection as an effective way to teach students the idea of history as struggle. History is about intersections, intersections are about choices, and choices influence struggle.

Having students recognize the element of choice is, however, only the first step. They next need to appreciate the consequences of the action or inaction relative to the other people waiting to enter the intersection. In the classic scenario, two or more cars have wrecked in a busy intersection. All parties claim the right of way. How do we reconstruct and determine how they came to rest as they did tangled in a twisted heap of metal, or in some cases with one vehicle totaled and the other mostly intact, or yet in other cases with both vehicles only lightly scratched?

If, for instance, we conceive of Booker T. Washington's 1895 Atlanta Exposition Speech as a critical juncture in U.S. race relations, how did his public acquiescence to the idea of separate but equal impact the struggle for racial equality? As the lead car, so to speak, how did Washington's memorable pledge, "in all things purely social we can be as separate as the fingers, yet one as the hand in all things essential to mutual progress," affect African Americans? Certainly, other Black leaders sitting at the same intersection, most notably W. E. B. DuBois, disagreed with Washington's decision to stay the course. Having students uncover Washington's motivations and reconstruct his arguments will help them to better understand the nature of the philosophical collision and rupture that later developed between him and other Black leaders, most notably DuBois, over the struggle for black equality in America.

The complex problem of working out these types of disagreements, disentangling the various sides, and understanding their relative positions is akin to accident reconstruction. In charging our students with the task of putting the pieces back together and explaining what led to the collision, we allow them to uncover history while engaging important questions like, What can this tell us about the historical process, about rights in conflict and the evolution of American democracy? How does it engage our larger understanding of history?

The Intersection and Teaching Core Democratic Values Through History

In looking at history through the lens of the Intersection, three important lessons emerge for students:

1. History does not occur in a vacuum.

2. Individuals make choices and thus have the power to shape the future.

3. Advancing the cause of freedom and democracy requires action.

All of these are consistent with the goals outlined by the National Council for the Social Studies (NCSS; 1991) of using content knowledge to teach students the importance and values of fulfilling the duties of citizenship, which require action in a participatory democracy.

According to NCSS, there are ten Core Democratic Values. The main principles of these values can be traced back (or historically fingerprinted; see Chapter 3) not only to our founding documents, such as the Declaration of Independence and the Constitution, but also to later documents, such as Lincoln's Gettysburg Address and the Civil Rights Act of 1964. The issues that often propel people into the Intersection arise from disputes over these Core Democratic Values. Consider the following and imagine the intersections that have arisen as Americans have tried to negotiate the rocky terrain associated with each value.

Core Democratic Values—Fundamental Beliefs

LIFE: The individual's right to life should be considered inviolable except in certain highly restricted and extreme circumstances, such as the use of deadly force to protect one's own or others' lives.

LIBERTY: The right to liberty is considered an unalterable aspect of the human condition. Central to this idea of liberty is the understanding that the political or personal obligations of parents or ancestors cannot be legitimately forced on people. The right to liberty includes *personal freedom*: the private realm in which the individual is free to act, to think and to believe, and which the government cannot legitimately invade; *political freedom*: the right to participate freely in the political process, choose and remove public officials, to be governed under a rule of law; the right to a free flow of information and ideas, open debate and right of assembly; and *economic freedom*: the right to acquire, use, transfer and dispose of private property without unreasonable governmental interference; the right to seek employment wherever one pleases; to change employment at will; and to engage in any lawful economic activity.

THE PURSUIT OF HAPPINESS: It is the right of citizens in the American constitutional democracy to attempt to attain—"pursue"—happiness in their own way, so long as they do not infringe upon the rights of others.

COMMON GOOD: The public or common good requires that individual citizens have the commitment and motivation—that they accept their obligation—to promote the welfare of the community and to work together with other members for the greater benefit of all.

JUSTICE: People should be treated fairly in the distribution of the benefits and burdens of society, the correction of wrongs and injuries, and in the gathering of information and making of decisions.

EQUALITY: All citizens have: political equality and are not denied these rights unless by due process of law; legal equality and should be treated as equals before the law; social equality so as there should be no class hierarchy sanctioned by law; economic equality which tends to strengthen political and social equality for extreme economic inequality tends to undermine all other forms of equality and should therefore be avoided.

DIVERSITY: Variety in culture and ethnic background, race, lifestyle, and belief is not only permissible but desirable and beneficial in a pluralist society.

TRUTH: Citizens can legitimately demand that truth-telling as refraining from lying and full disclosure by government be the rule, since trust in the veracity of government constitutes an essential element of the bond between governors and governed.

POPULAR SOVEREIGNTY: The citizenry is collectively the sovereign of the state and holds ultimate authority over public officials and their policies.

PATRIOTISM: Virtuous citizens display a devotion to their country, including devotion to the fundamental values upon which it depends.

Source: Quigley (1991)

Some of our most interesting and engaging units in history deal with these issues, and yet we often do not relate them back to these important core values. Likewise, teachers often do not use history to teach civics. In treating the two sister subjects as separate entities we miss the important point that our democratic values emerge from our history and are constantly being negotiated and renegotiated as we continue to work toward perfecting our democracy. Time and space are factors as well, as the meaning of each of these core values has grown and, in some cases, changed over time to include women and minorities, an expanded government bureaucracy, important innovations in science and technology, and new threats at home and abroad. This is part of the value of the Intersection as a teaching method. It allows you to make connections over time by looking at various issues in the Intersection. Consider the usual suspects—slavery, gender equality, civil rights, and American democratic principles—and the not so usual ones—immigration, judicial activism, and gun control. The Intersection can provide teachers with an effective strategy to enable students to understand conflict and the historical process.

One can clearly see such issues highlighted in historical content when using the Intersection. In the aftermath of the Civil War, for instance, every aspect of southern life, from politics to etiquette to labor, had to be renegotiated. However, these negotiations had to take into account the various positions and understandings of those positioned around the stoplight created by the end of the war. These negotiations took place in the Intersection, the crossroads where the vital interests of one group conflicted with interests or perceived rights of another. This played out in cities, hamlets, and farms throughout the South. Planters concerned with securing a cheap and dependable source of labor had to balance those concerns against the interests and demands of the freedmen and freedwomen who insisted on setting their own terms for work. Early attempts at segregation like the Black Codes, the debate over women's suffrage, and the transformation of southern labor via sharecropping, the crop lien system, and debt peonage are all examples of Intersections as the former slaves, laborers, and women all sought to assert their interest in this period. They illustrate the complex negotiations and interactions that shape history as well as the humanity of historical actors.

For example, Elizabeth Cady Stanton, abolitionist, freedom fighter, and suffragist, was also a human being who made choices, some good and some bad. As she and Susan B. Anthony pressed forward with demands that the nation recognize the rights of women, they found themselves parting company with former allies as issues and interests bifurcated in the aftermath of the war. They lobbied for women's rights, for instance, as the Radical Republicans in Congress, many of whom were former allies in the abolitionist movement, debated the extension of the right of suffrage regardless of race, color, or previous condition of servitude, but not gender. Ultimately denied the right to vote with the passage of the Fifteenth Amendment, Stanton spoke out. Exasperated by the denial of female suffrage, especially in light of the widespread political corruption of the day, Stanton attempted to exploit the all-too-common prejudice directed toward newly enfranchised blacks as well as other minority groups. Moving into the Intersection of the politics of racial exclusion, she implored the readers of a new radical periodical called *The Revolution* to recognize that certainly educated women of "wealth, refinement and culture" had more to contribute to the nation as informed voters than uneducated black men or recent foreign immigrants. Ignoring the fact that all women regardless of color had been denied the franchise, Stanton nevertheless settled on the issue of race. "If you do not wish the lower orders of Chinese, Africans, Germans and Irish, with their low ideals of womanhood, to make laws for you and your daughters," Stanton warned her readers in a strongly worded appeal, "awake to the present danger and demand that women too be given the vote" (DuBois, 1978, p. 178). Stanton's stand on the issue illustrates the multiple intersections created by the passage of the Fifteenth Amendment.

SETTING UP THE INTERSECTION

One of the reasons the strategy of the Intersection works well with young people is the nature of their lives between the fifth and twelfth grades. Simply put, their whole lives are about intersections. As they try to balance the various demands placed on their time, develop a sense of belonging, and test the boundaries of parental authority, or even our patience in class, they are negotiating intersections. The choices they make often impact others, even if they are not aware of the immediate consequences. Once introduced to the concept of the Intersection, they can easily apply it to their daily interaction with peers, parents, teachers, coaches, and friends. This inevitably helps the students to develop a sense of historical empathy in line with the Bradley Commission's (1995) habits of the mind, which are listed in the Introduction. Using the concept of the Intersection will help you engage most if not all of the 13 habits of the mind identified by the Commission.

How do you begin to use the strategy of the Intersection? In the classic intersection scenario, for each side sitting at the non-working lights, there are decisions. In order to stimulate critical thinking, ask your students to consider the full range of these decisions for each side. Follow these steps:

1. Conceptualize a historical problem like a traffic accident about to happen.

2. Place the various historical figures or groups involved at the different non-working lights.

3. There should be at least three sides.

4. Assign them colors that correspond with their relative positions.
   - Green: The side that wants things to change (go)
   - Red: The side that wants things to remain the same (stop)
   - Yellow: Those trapped at the light on caution

5. Select either a single primary source for the class that represents all sides or several sources that illustrate the various positions of each group (see below for suggestions).

6. Have the students in each group read the document and then prepare a list of reasons explaining their relative position: go, caution, or stop.

7. Reconvene the class. Have each group present its position, and then have the students debate their positions. Give each side enough time to articulate its position at the traffic light.

8. (Optional) After the debate has ended, switch sides and ask the various groups to defend a position other than their own.

9. After they have thoroughly discussed each side, ask them to prepare a brief writing exercise that looks at the issue from all sides.

A SAMPLING OF HISTORICAL INTERSECTIONS

In history, intersections occur in the space where theory meets practice, where rights come into conflict, where expectations do not match reality— in short, where people inevitably must negotiate and decide critical issues. Let us look at some examples.

PFDA: A Progressive Era Intersection

A good example of the intersection at work is the circumstances leading to the passage of the Pure Food and Drug Act (PFDA) in 1906. That year author Upton Sinclair moved into the Intersection to try to expose what he saw as the inhumane treatment of working people in America. As a socialist, he dreamed of a society in which everyone would be treated equally without distinction of wealth. By exposing the harsh and unsanitary conditions in which they labored, he hoped to bring about change. He used his writing as a means to address this issue. The publication of his novel *The Jungle* in 1906 ushered in a wave of reform, although not necessarily in the way he expected. After it caught the attention of high-level government officials, including President Theodore Roosevelt, it inspired the passage of the Pure Food and Drug Act addressing issues in sanitation but not the plight of workers as Sinclair had hoped. Sinclair later famously lamented that he had "aimed for the readers' hearts, but hit them in the stomach."

At its core, however, it is a classic example of the Intersection. Sinclair was not the only one on go. In actuality there had been movement toward inspections before his novel. One of the reasons Sinclair may have missed his mark is because his treatment of the unsanitary conditions in the meatpacking industry coincided with the interest of big business, whom he detested. Issues of sanitation had long been on the industry radar. Dating back to the 1870s concerns over the safety of American meat exports had left Europeans queasy about importations. In order to address this issue, the larger meat manufacturers including Swift, Armour, Cudahy, and Morris lobbied state officials to increase inspections. This Big Four derived at least three tangible benefits from the proposed inspections. First, they addressed European concerns, creating opportunities for greater exports. Next, they helped to tamp down and eliminate as a source of competition smaller companies, who in their desire to compete often cut corners in production. Last, they addressed issues of safety at home. For very different reasons, they joined Sinclair on go at the Intersection in 1906. Smaller operations were likely more cautious or even opposed to inspections while state, local, and federal officials ran the gamut from progressive reformers like Roosevelt who advocated reform to some members of Congress who challenged the constitutionality of the proposed law.

Such accounts bring life to the issues of yesteryear in ways that demonstrate the rich complexity of history. While students would most likely see all business as being opposed to regulation, the concept of the Intersection introduces the interplay of interest and action in a way that is easily understandable and can generate a good deal of discussion in response to the following questions:

- Who was on go? Who wanted things to change and why? What issues did they bring with them into the intersection?
- Who was on stop? Why were they resistant to change? What fears, concerns did they offer for their opposition to change?
- Who was on caution? What issues concerned them?

This lesson on the PFDA correlates with the National Standards for History (National Center for History in the Schools, 1996) Era 7—The Emergence of Modern America (1890–1930):

STANDARD 1: How Progressives and others addressed problems of industrial capitalism, urbanization, and political corruption.

Standard 1A: The student understands the origin of the Progressives and the coalitions they formed to deal with issues at the local and state level.

7–12: Explain how intellectuals and religious leaders laid the groundwork and publicists spread the word for Progressive plans to reform American society.

9–12: Assess Progressive efforts to regulate big business, curb labor militancy, and protect the rights of workers and consumers.

At the end of this unit, students should be able to identify the following of the Bradley Commission's (1995) Habits of the Mind:

8. Grasp the complexity of historical causation, respect particularity, and avoid excessively abstract generalizations.

9. Appreciate the often-tentative nature of judgments about the past, and thereby avoid the temptation to seize upon particular "lessons" or history as cures for present ills.

10. Recognize the importance of individuals who have made a difference in history, and the significance of personal character for both good and ill.

11. Appreciate the force of the nonrational, the irrational, the accidental, in history and human affairs.

Lincoln and Fremont at the Intersection

Here is an example of a Historical Intersection using President Lincoln's appointment of John C. Fremont.

In 1861, Lincoln's war plans collided with the will of one of his commanders in the field, John C. Fremont. In July of that year, Lincoln appointed the celebrated explorer, nicknamed the "Pathfinder," as the commander of the volatile Western Department. Fremont seemed an ideal choice. Lincoln thought that Fremont's popularity might boost Union sentiment in the Trans Mississippi Territories including the vital border state of Missouri that was under assault from pro-secessionist agitators.

Exacerbated by the situation in Missouri, a little over a month into his command Fremont decided to place the entire state under martial law. Convinced that some type of direct blow to slavery in the region would undermine the opposition, on August 30 Fremont decreed that all slaves in the state belonging to secessionists were henceforth and forevermore free.

Informed of Fremont's actions, Lincoln was understandably concerned. Not only had Fremont exceeded his authority, his actions threatened to compromise the fragile bond between the government and the slave-owning border states that had remained loyal and in the Union. He immediately contacted his commander and asked him to modify his order to conform to the First Confiscation Act that only emancipated the slaves of owners who directly aided the Confederacy. Fremont, however, refused.

The situation created a serious dilemma for the president. Torn between alienating the Radical Republicans to whom he owed his election and the moderates in the state whose support he would need to maintain Missouri for the Union, Lincoln pursued a more cautious policy. Although he agreed with Fremont in principle, he believed that such a dramatic policy required Union victories. After allowing a few weeks for the hullabaloo to subside, the president stripped Fremont of his command and revoked his proclamation, but not before the president was subjected to a thrashing in the press on his reprimand of Fremont and the issue of slavery. The episode nonetheless served to heighten the nation's concerns over the abolition of slavery and how it would be accomplished. Lincoln's slow-but-steady course was politically wiser. In this scenario, while Fremont was clearly on go with regard to emancipation, Lincoln was more cautious. As president he had to balance the varied interests of Missourians and others who would have viewed such a move as too radical.

Another useful aspect of the Intersection as a teaching tool is the ability to relate the complexity of issues and varying positions. Abraham Lincoln may have been on caution about abolishing slavery too soon, but he felt pressure from members of his party and his military commanders who were on go and advocated more immediate action. Anyone who has ever sat in traffic understands this phenomenon. The choruses of beeps from the vehicles behind the lead car demand action, even as the leader carefully weighs what he or she considers the best course. As Lincoln felt pressure about emancipation, he pressured General McClellan, cautious about military strategy for a decisive victory. In this sense, Intersections always create and affect other Intersections. If there was still some ambiguity on the part of politicians regarding abolition, for instance, the slaves themselves had no trouble interpreting the meaning of the war. For them it was about freedom, pure and simple, and they acted accordingly, as shown in the next example of a Historical Intersection.

The Emancipation Proclamation in the Intersection

Historians have long debated the force of the Emancipation Proclamation and its impact on slavery. This unit is designed to have students look at this problem through the lens of the Intersection. The three documents in this case are

1. Lincoln's Emancipation Proclamation (1863),

2. Two letters (1864) from a Missouri Black soldier, Spotswood Rice, to his daughters and to their owner,

3. The Thirteenth Amendment to the Constitution (1865).

The Rice letters are important because they fall in between the Emancipation Proclamation, which freed the slaves in those states in active rebellion against the Union, and the Thirteenth Amendment that abolished slavery. Rice's understanding of his freedom as articulated in these letters is important because it reveals him moving into the Intersection to demand freedom for his enslaved daughters as well. As the students read the letters, ask them to think about the following:

- How did Rice's decision to act create Intersections with his military commanders, his fellow soldiers, his children, the Lincoln Administration, and, most important, his former owner?
- In what ways did the language of the Emancipation Proclamation encourage Rice's belief that slavery was on its deathbed and that he had an ally in support of its abolition in the government?
- In what ways could Rice's actions have proved problematic for the Lincoln Administration?
- Where do you think certain people mentioned by Rice in the letters fit at the traffic lights?

Letters From Spotswood Rice

[Benton Barracks Hospital, St. Louis, Mo. September 3, 1864]

I received a leteter from Cariline telling me that you say I tried to steal to plunder my child away from you now I want you to understand that mary is my Child and she is a

God given rite of my own and you may hold on to hear as long as you can but I want you to remembor this one thing that the longor you keep my Child from me the longor you will have to burn in hell and the qwicer youll get their for we are now makeing up a bout one thoughsand blacke troops to Come up tharough and wont to come through Glasgow and when we come wo be to Copperhood rabbels and to the Slaveholding rebbels for we dont expect to leave them there root neor branch but we thinke how ever that we that have Children in the hands of you devels we will trie your [vertues?] the day that we enter Glasgow I want you to understand kittey diggs that where ever you and I meets we are enmays to each orthere I offered once to pay you forty dollers for my own Child but I am glad now that you did not accept it Just hold on now as long as you can and the worse it will be for you you never in you life befor I came down hear did you give Children any thing not eny thing whatever not even a dollers worth of expencs now you call my children your pro[per]ty not so with me my Children is my own and I expect to get them and when I get ready to come after mary I will have bout a powrer and autherity to bring hear away and to exacute vengencens on them that holds my Child you will then know how to talke to me I will assure that and you will know how to talk rite too I want you now to just hold on to hear if you want to iff your conchosence tells thats the road go that road and what it will brig you to kittey diggs I have no fears about geting mary out of your hands this whole Government gives chear to me and you cannot help your self

Spotswood Rice

Source: Spotswood Rice to Kittey Diggs, [3 Sept. 1864], enclosed in F. W. Diggs to Genl. Rosecrans, 10 Sept. 1864, D-296 1864, Letters Received, ser. 2593, Dept. of the MO, U.S. Army Continental Commands, Record Group 393 Pt. 1, National Archives.

[Benton Barracks Hospital, St. Louis, Mo. September 3, 1864]

My Children I take my pen in hand to rite you A few lines to let you know that I have not forgot you and that I want to see you as bad as ever now my Dear Children I want you to be contented with whatever may be your lots be assured that I will have you if it cost me my life on the 28th of the mounth. 8 hundred White and 8 hundred blacke solders expects to start up the rivore to Glasgow and above there thats to be jeneraled by a jeneral that will give me both of you when they Come I expect to be with, them and expect to get you both in return. Dont be uneasy my children I expect to have you. If Diggs dont give you up this Government will and I feel confident that I will get you Your Miss Kaitty said that I tried to steal you But I'll let her know that god never intended for man to steal his own flesh and blood. If I had no cofidence in God I could have confidence in her But as it is If I ever had any Confidence in her I have none now and never expect to have And I want her to remember if she meets me with ten thousand soldiers she [will?] meet her enemy I once [thought] that I had some respect for them but now my respects is worn out and have no sympathy for Slaveholders. And as for her cristianantty I expect the Devil has Such in hell You tell her from me that She is the frist Christian that I ever hard say that aman could Steal his own child especially out of human bondage

You can tell her that She can hold to you as long as she can I never would expect to ask her again to let you come to me because I know that the devil has got her hot set againsts that that is write now my Dear children I am a going to close my letter to you Give my love to all enquiring friends tell them all that we are well and want to see them very much and Corra and Mary receive the greater part of it you sefves and dont think hard of us not sending you any thing I you father have a plenty for you when I see you Spott & Noah sends their love to both of you Oh! My Dear children how I do want to see you

Spotswood Rice

Source: [Spotswood Rice] to My Children, [3 Sept. 1864], enclosed in F. W. Diggs to Genl. Rosecrans, 10 Sept. 1864, D-296 1864, Letters Received, ser. 2593, Dept. of the MO, U.S. Army Continental Commands, Record Group 393 Pt. 1, National Archives.

After the students read the letters, ask them to decide where to place the major players. Here is my interpretation:

- *Green light:* Spotswood Rice
- *Red light:* Kitty Diggs
- *Yellow:* Spot, Noah, Mary, anyone else? (I placed Spotswood Rice's children here based on his instructions for them to "be contented with whatever may be your lots." Clearly Rice hoped that they would stay on the plantation where he would be able to find and free them. Others in your class may see this differently, which should make for lively debate and discussion.)

Go deeper and ask the students to think about where to place the various other historical actors in the Intersection. Where would you place the Lincoln Administration or Rice's commanders?

Adding Layers

Consider the same exercise with two adaptations, first with a political cartoon and next as a document-based CSI Cold Case on Lincoln and the Emancipation Proclamation.

The title and date of the cartoon shown in Figure 4.1 add yet another layer to the exercise. The cartoonist likens emancipation to a raffle where the winner's reward is a seemingly useless prize. Using this cartoon as the starting point, you could easily have your students consider the important impact that slaves turned soldiers had on the war. In his book *The Negro's Civil War*, historian James McPherson (1965), for example, argued that Black soldiers helped to tip the balance in favor of the Union. Nevertheless, he

FIGURE 4.1   "The Man Who Won the Elephant at the Raffl"

THE MAN WHO WON THE ELEPHANT AT THE RAFFLE.
Gen. Weitzel.—"BUT THE QUESTION IS, WHAT AM I TO DO WITH THE CREATURE?"
[See Gen. Weitzel's Report to Gen. Butler, on capturing several hundred wagon-loads of Niggers.]

Source: Civil War Cartoon Collection, American Antiquarian Society, January 1863.

maintained that their military service would not have been possible without Lincoln's decision to issue the Emancipation Proclamation. Other scholars such as Ira Berlin (1992), Barbara Fields (1990), and Vincent Harding (1981) have argued that the slaves were agents of their own deliverance as their actions put pressure on the Lincoln Administration to deal immediately with the elephant in the room, slavery, even as he plotted a more cautious course.

Eisenhower and Warren at the Intersection

Used in conjunction with Historical Fingerprinting (see Chapter 3), Intersections provide fertile opportunities for students to appreciate Crossovers and the Bifurcation of issues. Political scientist Frederick Lee Morton (1988) has observed, "Appointment by the President is no guarantee that he will be pleased by the results. American history is strewn with examples of presidents who came to regret their judicial appointments" (p. 171). As an illustration, consider Dwight David Eisenhower's appointment of Earl Warren to the United States Supreme Court in 1953. How would you design a unit using the concept of the Intersection to look at the battle over school desegregation in the 1950s? How might you incorporate the Morton quote as well? In constructing this unit, I suggest that you emphasize the four Bradley Commission's (1995) habits of the mind listed in the PDFA example earlier in this chapter. They are central to most exercises using the Intersection.

In September 1957, the efforts of nine Black students to integrate Central High School in Little Rock Arkansas transfixed the nation, but some would argue that the circumstances leading to the showdown in Little Rock began long before with a presidential appointment in 1953. In that year, president Dwight David Eisenhower named Earl Warren to replace Supreme Court chief justice Fred Vinson, who had died. Eisenhower assumed that Warren, the former governor from California and vice presidential nominee for the Republican Party, would be a rock of stability, but later called the appointment "the biggest damn-fool mistake I ever made." A staunch conservative at the time of his appointment, Warren became a liberal on the bench, spearheading an activist court that handed down several landmark rulings including *Brown v. Board of Education* and *Miranda v. Arizona.* As a mark of Warren's and his fellow justices' resolve to deal with the issue of school desegregation, the Court met in special session in the summer of 1958 to hear the case of *Cooper v. Aaron* to avoid further delay in the implementation of the Brown decision.

The Warren Court's judicial activism forced the president, who had been lukewarm on Civil Rights, into the Intersection as he was increasingly called upon to enforce its decrees. While he privately stewed over the Court's decision in *Brown v. Board of Education,* when it came time to deal with state officials like Arkansas governor Orval Faubus, who sought to defy the Court's ruling pledging that "blood would run in the streets of Little Rock," Eisenhower upheld his duty to enforce the law. While Faubus only had to answer to his constituents, Eisenhower had the whole of history and the nation to consider. He justified his actions (his reasons for entering the Intersection to prevent a pileup in Arkansas) during a televised address on September 24, 1957. "At a time when we face grave situations abroad," he explained, "because of the hatred that communism bears toward a system of government based on human rights, it would be difficult to exaggerate the harm that is being done to the prestige and influence and indeed to the safety of our nation and the world." "Our enemies are gloating over this incident," he continued, "and using it everywhere to misrepresent our whole nation. We are portrayed as a violator of those standards which the peoples of the world united to proclaim in the Charter of the United Nations" (Lawson & Payne, 1998, p. 69).

Having students go through the exercise of examining the various considerations and circumstances that led to the showdown in Little Rock demonstrates the value of historical accident reconstruction as a teaching tool. President of the Arkansas NAACP Conference of Branches Daisy Bates and the brave students who made up the Little Rock nine were not the only ones who had to make difficult decisions. The entire episode illustrates how Intersections are negotiated and renegotiated in the process of history. At every level, as the participants in the drama moved closer and closer to the start of school in September 1957, their decisions influenced and affected the actions and reactions of others.

One of the persons rarely credited for his role in helping to avert a greater disaster, for example, is Little Rock mayor Woodrow Wilson Mann. Unlike Governor Faubus, Mann welcomed desegregation as an important step in affirming American democracy. Elected mayor of the city in 1955, he quickly moved into the Intersection created by the Court's decisions in the Brown case and the bus boycott in Montgomery, setting about dismantling many of the vestiges of Jim Crow in the state capital including ending segregation on city buses. After watching tensions build in the weeks leading up to the confrontation, on September 24 Mann sent the president an urgent communication asking him to send federal troops "in the interest of humanity, law and order." Mann, like so many other little known players in history, represents the importance of agency and that actions really do have consequences.

The following is the way the persons at the Little Rock Intersection could be labeled:

- *Red light:* Governor Faubus
- *Green light:* Daisy Bates, mayor Woodrow Wilson Mann, and the Little Rock nine (Minnijean Brown, Elizabeth Echford, Ernest Green, Thelma Mothershed, Melba Patillo Beals, Gloria Ray, Terrence Roberts, Jefferson Thomas, Carlotta Walls)
- *Yellow light:* At least initially President Eisenhower, the National Guard

This is another good example of how to use the idea of Intersections as a teaching method with your students.

Gun Control in the Intersection

The issue of gun control and the political career of Ronald Reagan is a great civics lesson packaged with important historical content that incorporates many of the core civic values identified by NCSS (as listed earlier in this chapter).

As part of the Bill of Rights, the Founders included the Second Amendment that maintained, "A well regulated militia, being necessary to the security of a free state, the right of the people to keep and bear arms, shall not be infringed." Throughout the course of American history, these words have fueled debate and thrust various individuals and groups into the Intersection as they have argued for the extension and restriction of gun ownership as essential to American democracy. Imagine a joint history and civics lesson that asks students to consider the issue of gun control with historical content as the conduit for learning.

On May 2, 1967, an armed group of twenty-four men and six women interrupted a session of the California legislature. The group, part of the Black Panther Party for Self Defense (BPP), traveled to Sacramento to register their protest against a bill, authored by representative Donald Mulford, under consideration "prohibiting the carrying of firearms on one's person or in a vehicle, in any public place or on any public street." Specifically drafted to deal with the Panthers, who, following their creation in October of 1966, instituted armed patrols of the police in hopes of decreasing acts of police brutality, the bill was hotly contested. The Panthers' use of the gun had already made them center stage in a debate in California. The Mulford protest shined a national spotlight on the BPP. The organization had stepped into the Intersection, the crossroads of history where the actions and reactions of those seeking to advance or maintain a particular position are worked out. In United States history, this most often occurs in periods of crisis when underlying disagreements over our democratic ideals, most notably of liberty and equality, come into conflict with the reality of our everyday practices.

In the case of the Black Panthers in 1967, issues of civil rights, gun control, police brutality, and racial equality intersected in Sacramento. On the one hand, the BPP sought to insure its Second Amendment rights to continue its armed patrols of the police, in protest against what they perceived as a dual system of justice for people of color in Oakland. On the other hand, the legislature worked to ensure the safety and security of California's law enforcement officers against what they perceived as a dangerous if not unlawful threat, considering that at the time of BPP's march on the state capital, the frontier tradition of carrying arms was still permitted in the Golden State.

Although the Panthers intended to use their protest to highlight the injustice of the Mulford bill as directed against them, the protest had the opposite impact. The Panthers claimed their right of self-defense to protect against police brutality in the African American community. In a period where civil rights protests, anti-war protests, and long hot riotous summers took center stage and where two political assassinations, those of John F. Kennedy and Malcolm X, had already left the nation reeling, the actions of the California legislature were understandable. A month after the protest California governor Ronald Reagan signed the Mulford Act of 1967 into law, affecting not only the BPP but also all gun owners in the state.

Fourteen years after signing the Mulford Act, and sixty-nine days into his Presidency, Reagan would again find himself at the center of the national debate on gun control after he sustained serious injuries along with an aide, James Brady, in a failed assassination attempt. In spite of significant opposition within his own party, Reagan went on to champion the Brady bill, which, for its time, was one of the most comprehensive and restrictive pieces of gun control legislation.

This is a great case study because it demonstrates how teachers can wed a discussion of civics and NCSS' core democratic values with important historical content through the use of the Intersection as a teaching method.

QUESTIONS FOR REVIEW AND REFLECTION

1. After reading the chapter how would you define the concept of the intersection? How about agency? Spend a few minutes thinking about how you might explain these concepts to your students? What examples might you use to communicate these concepts to your students?

2. Military conflict often creates unexpected intersections. This chapter focuses heavily on intersections created by the Civil War. What are some other military conflicts that have produced important social, economic, political, and cultural intersections? How might you go about preparing to discuss similar intersections in other foreign and domestic conflicts?

3. Students are often better able to understand historic events when they are able to relate them to present issues. What present issues and debates (i.e., immigration reform, same-sex marriage) are creating intersections for Americans? How might you use these in the classroom to introduce the idea of the intersection in history?

REFERENCES

Berlin, I., Fields, B., Miller, S. F., Reidy, J. P. & Rowland, L. S. (Eds.). (1992). *Free at last: A documentary history of slavery, freedom, and the Civil War* (pp. 480–482). New York: The New Press.

Bradley Commission on History in Schools. (1989). Building a history curriculum: Guidelines for teaching history in schools. *The History Teacher, 23*, 7–35.

Drake, F. & Nelson, L. (2004). *Engagement in teaching history.* Upper Saddle River, NJ: Pearson.

DuBois, E. C. (1978). *Feminism and suffrage: The emergence of an independent women's movement in America 1848-1869.* Ithaca, NY: Cornell University Press.

Fields, B. J. (1990). Who freed the slaves? In G. C. Ward (Ed.), *The Civil War: An illustrated history* (pp. 178–181). New York: Knopf.

Foltz, R. C. (2003). Does nature have historical agency? World history, environmental history, and how historians can help save the planet. *The History Teacher, 37*, 57 pars. Retrieved December 31, 2007, from http://www.historycooperative.org/journals/ht/37.1/foltz.html

Harding, V. (1981). *There is a river: The Black struggle for freedom in America.* New York: Harcourt Brace Jovanovich.

Lawson, S. F. & Payne, C. (1998). *Debating the civil rights movement, 1945–1968.* Lanham, MD: Rowman & Littlefield Publishers.

McPherson, J. (1965). The Negro's Civil War: How American Negroes felt and acted during the war for the Union. New York: Pantheon Books.

Morton, F. L. (1988). Conservatives in the courts in United States and Canada. In B. Cooper, A. Kornberg, & W. Mishler (Eds.). *The resurgence of conservatism in Anglo-American democracies.* Durham, NC: Duke University Press.

National Center for History in the Schools. 1996. *National standards for history* [Electronic version]. Los Angeles: Author.

National Council for the Social Studies. (n.d.) *About NCSS.* Retrieved March 20, 2008, from http://www.socialstudies.org/about/

Quigley, C. N. (Ed.) *Civitas: A framework for civic education.* [National Council for the Social Studies Bulletin No. 86]. Calabasas, CA: Center for Civic Education.

Sinclair, U. (1906). *The Jungle.* New York: Doubleday.

National Advisory Commission on Civil Disorders (Kerner Commission). (1968). *Report of the National Advisory Commission on Civil Disorders.* Washington DC: U.S. Government Printing Office.

RESOURCES AND FURTHER READING

Brown, S. D. & Drake, F. D. (2005). History in education for citizenship in a democracy. *International Journal of Social Education, 20(2)*, 13–34.

In this stimulating article Drake and Brown make a strong case for why history should be an integral part of civics and government courses, and vice versa. This is a good place to begin thinking about ways to infuse your history instruction with civics and government, like the application of the Core Democratic Values from NCSS discussed in this chapter.

DeConde, A. (2001). *Gun violence in America: The struggle for control.* Boston: Northeastern University Press.

This book provides a fairly comprehensive overview of the debate over gun control by a noted political scientist that treats the subject by examining the political, social, and legal collisions that have occurred over competing interpretations of the Second Amendment.

Duvall, J. M. (2002). Processes of elimination: Progressive-era hygienic ideology, waste, and Upton Sinclair's *The Jungle. American Studies 43(3)*, 29–56.

This is good article that links Upton Sinclair's *Jungle* to Progressive Era reform, and an ideal starting place for those interested in teaching this aspect of Progressive reform.

Hakim, J. (2006). Choosing five Americans who got it right, or history for young minds. *Magazine of History, 20,* 12–16.

In this delightful article Joy Hakim profiles the lives of five Americans, including Roger Williams and Ida B. Wells, who stood in defense of their principles. This is a great place to start thinking about how to use the concept of the Intersection in teaching history.

Parrish, W. E. (1978). Fremont in Missouri. *Civil War Times Illustrated, 17(1),* 4–10, 40–45.

This is a good short article for building content knowledge on John C. Fremont. The article is also student friendly and could easily be assigned to middle and high school students.

Patrick, J. J., & Leming, R. S. (Eds.). (2001). *Principles and practices of democracy in the education of social studies teachers. Civic Learning in Teacher Education.* Bloomington, IN: ERIC Clearinghouse for Social Studies/Social Science Education.

This valuable collection of essays grew out of a conference co-sponsored by the Center for Civic Education (California) and the Social Studies Development Center (Indiana). While the central theme of the conference centered on education for democratic citizenship of prospective social studies teachers, the essays collectively offer fresh insights and valuable methods for teaching civics, history and the social studies.

Tap, B. (1994). Reconstructing emancipation's martyr: John C. Fremont and the Joint Committee on the Conduct of the War. *Gateway Heritage, 14(4)*, 36–53.

This is another good source of background on Fremont. It can double as a student reading; however, it is much more appropriate for high school students because of the length and some of the vocabulary.

Thompson, W. F. Jr. (1965). Pictorial images of the Negro during the Civil War. *Wisconsin Magazine of History, 48(4)*, 282–294.

This is a good source for images related to African Americans and the Civil War.

Volpe, V. L. (1994). The Fremonts and emancipation in Missouri. *Historian, 56*, 339–354.

Let this be your starting place for building teacher background knowledge on Fremont and emancipation in Missouri.

Williams, Y. (1998). In the name of the law: The 1967 shooting of Huey Newton and law enforcement's permissive environment. *Negro History Bulletin, 61(2)*, 6–18.

This short article on the birth of the Black Panther Party also details the Panthers' march on the state capital in 1967 to protest the Mulford Act. Given the multiple intersections, including the quest for equal rights, black power, and the right to bear arms, this is also a good place to begin thinking about teaching agency and intersections as they pertain to the struggle for civil rights and Black power in the United States in the late 1960s.

5

Meet SCOTUS

Engaging Students in the Drama of Court Cases

The well-told story about the national past should always be an argument,
a thesis, an analysis disguised in the action and drama of its narrative.

—David Levering Lewis

In 1993, the nation was transfixed with the O. J. Simpson trial and with forensic science. For more than a few days I barely made it to my graduate classes and adjusted my schedule to fit the testimony of crime scene investigator Dennis Fung and his subsequent cross-examination by renowned attorney and DNA expert Barry Scheck. I was riveted. The rest of the trial, save the verdict, failed to elicit the same interest from me, and a few weeks later I was settled back into my normal routine.

There is something magical about courtroom drama. Legal contests involve all the areas we engage as history and social studies educators, from research to weighing evidence to making arguments based on the evidence in search of favorable judgment of our interpretation of some past event. Although some see court cases as a departure from the standard narrative of history, lurking behind the cold stark facts of every court case is a much larger story awaiting rediscovery and a forgotten Intersection waiting to be explored.

WHAT IS SCOTUS?

Few of the rights that we enjoy as citizens have escaped debate and or adjudication in our courts of law. It is not only intellectually challenging but also fun to cast students in the roles of historic figures who found themselves at the center of judicial maelstroms. Students generally appreciate the opportunity to prepare and make oral arguments in class. By entering into dialogue and debate with one another and those in the past, they can experience vicariously the intersection of principle versus practice. They can also see more clearly how our judicial system works. Finally yet importantly, the trial itself is a true exhibition of what they have learned.

As Grant Wiggins and Jay McTighe (1998) observe,

> The problems that we develop for students should be as close as possible to the situation in which a scholar, artist, engineer, or other professional attacks such problems. The time allowed and conditions of work, for example, should be as far away as possible from the typical controlled exam situation. If understanding is to blossom, students need to have a clear performance goal and be required to keep that goal in constant view as they work. The case method in law and the problem based learning method in medicine exemplify this point. (p. 94)

The creative use of court cases in history classes follows the recommendations of Wiggins and McTighe.

Encouraging Critical Thinking

With court cases, especially ones designed to encourage critical thinking, the teacher can easily touch on the three foundations of the historical process, namely the importance of biography, chronology, and the interpretation of evidence.

To provide an adequate defense of their client, students need to become very familiar with his or her life and work. This by definition requires them to research the person thoroughly. I usually put three or four books on reserve in the library along with a few short articles to help students build this all-important background content knowledge. In conjunction with Historical Fingerprinting (see Chapter 3), the first stages of building a case address the issues of Island and Core. What is unique about the person we are studying, her background, her experiences, etc.? What is the Core of her argument? Finally, just how did she come to make this argument?

Laying the foundation for the prosecution is no less daunting a task. In building a case for the state, students need to familiarize themselves with not only the people involved, but also oftentimes state, local, or federal policies that helped to bring about the litigation.

As students research court cases, I emphasize that the evidence binds the historian in so much as even a liberal interpretation of that evidence must be documented. This again is one of the great things about using court cases and crime scenes. They get students thinking critically about evidence and arguments in a way that helps them understand the ways in which pieces of evidence come together to make a historical argument. They have a premise, which they must support with facts. Although they can use other historians as expert witnesses in support of their thesis or challenge the testimony of such experts in constructing their own argument, essential to both is their review and understanding of the evidence.

While a number of my students struggled early on in preparing their case positions, their individual and collective growth over the course of the semester never ceased to amaze me. They morphed from passive recipients of knowledge to intellectual advocates comfortable enough in their understanding to engage others. A parent cornered me on back to school night, effusive with praise for the class, especially the trials. "I don't know what kind of magic you have," she exclaimed, "but all she talks about is history. Everything relates back to history. Her father is a police officer, and she even debates the law with him at dinner. He is so ecstatic!"

Such praise, however, only came after I worked out the bugs in my approach. My first year of teaching eleventh grade U.S. history, I ambitiously planned to assign 15 cases, including *Marbury v. Madison, Cherokee Nation v. Georgia,* and *Brown v. Board of Education,* hoping to open up the world of the law and its impact on history to the students. Still traditional in my view of the law, as I assigned each case I provided the students with edited copies of the decision and required them to prepare modified briefs. In addition, I asked them to memorize the first sections of the First, Fifth, and Fourteenth Amendments to the Constitution, assuming that this would help them in their briefs and in class discussions since the majority of the cases dealt with issues that touched on these important Amendments. The approach proved to be a disaster. While some parents truly appreciated the idea, they felt that the workload was far beyond eleventh graders. Moreover, while some students flourished, the vast majority treated the preparation of the briefs like a chore. Far from encouraging vigorous discussion, most days getting students to discuss the cases, in spite of the briefs, was about as easy, and enjoyable, as a trip to the dentist.

Introducing SCOTUS

Exhausted and exacerbated, during the winter recess I decided to restructure this part of the course. I scrapped the preparation of briefs, and for the remaining cases I selected three trials, *Murray v. Maryland, Korematsu v. United States,* and *Brandenburg v. Ohio.* When I shared my plan with one of my colleagues, she was a bit skeptical. "You mean you're not going to discuss *Brown v. Board of Education?*" she inquired. "Of course, I will," I replied, doing my best to look confident, "just not in the way I would normally do it."

When the students returned from break, I placed a picture of a cartoon character in judicial robes near the light switch. Above his head were the letters SCOTUS. "What's with Mr. Magoo?" one of the boys asked as he filed back toward his seat. I smiled. "That's not Mr. Magoo," I replied, "It's SCOTUS. He will be joining us for the second half of the semester." "No," said another student near the front, "that is Mr. Magoo. He was on a TV special before break. He can't see, and he is always bumping into stuff and saying, 'Oh, Magoo, you've done it again.'" Everyone laughed at the impromptu impression. I explained that SCOTUS stood for the Supreme Court of the United States, and we would be visiting him on occasion when we had legal questions. I explained the rules for presenting issues to SCOTUS using the Supreme Court's original and appellate jurisdiction. Finally, I told the students what SCOTUS says goes; he is the law of the land. You can disagree with him, but your only alternative is to turn to the legislative branch to enact legislation more harmonious with the Court's decision.

A few days later, I would come to appreciate the Mr. Magoo reference. We were discussing the Reconstruction era and the role of the Supreme Court in limiting the effectiveness of the Civil War amendments. The day before we had read the Civil Rights Acts of 1875, and for homework I handed out the facts in the collection of cases that constituted the Civil Rights Cases of 1883. In class we read Henry McNeil Turner's famous reaction to the cases, which he compared with the Dred Scott decision. "This is so unfair," one of the girls complained. "Why couldn't the judges see what impact this would have on the former slaves?" "Because sometimes, justice is blind," one of her classmates responded. "Somewhat like Mr. Magoo," she explained to a chorus of chuckles, "sometimes the Court interprets the law very narrowly and does not consider other factors." "This," I chimed in, "is called strict construction. It means that the court interprets the Constitution according to what it says." "So justice isn't really blind," explained the same student, "sometimes it needs glasses in order to help it see the issues more clearly." "Those glasses are the arguments that lawyers bring before the court," I continued, "issues that the framers of the law may not have considered that later might be seen as counter to the spirit and letter of the Constitution."

For the rest of the year SCOTUS became an integral part of the class. What would SCOTUS say about women demanding the right to vote? The exercise became more of a dialogue because the questions were generated by the students' own interest in relation to what we studied. They also began to reference the Court more when we encountered difficult issues in class. When we got to federal policies toward the Native Americans from the1870s to the 1890s, for instance, the students got into a spirited debate over the treatment of the Native peoples. "How could they do this," asked one student, "this was their land first." "Remember the Fourteenth Amendment," another advised. "They were not citizens under the language of the Amendment. Remember when we did that Cherokee case," she continued, "the courts called them domestic dependent nations so technically they could treat them like other countries and sign bad treaties with them." "African Americans were citizens," was the rebuttal from another student, "and they were mistreated as well. How do you explain that?" "*Plessy*," responded "Constance Baker Motley," one of the students whom I nicknamed after the famous African American jurist. In fact, I gave all of my students names of famous lawyers and justices, assuming that this would pique their curiosity and they might actually look the person up. The vast majority did, and some like Constance made it their mission to be like that lawyer in terms of the types of issues they engaged. "The court created a test for the separation of Blacks from Whites in *Plessy*," she continued. "That was the Court's doctrine of separate but equal." The students also began to describe their "judicial views" as strict construction or loose interpretation. This was perhaps the most gratifying part of these discussions because I could see the students claiming ownership over the knowledge and putting it to use much like Constance.

USING SCOTUS

As you are preparing to put together your mock trial here are some things to consider. No matter how engaging the subject matter, limit your actual class time to one or two periods. Also make sure you provide plenty of resources for student research, especially on old or obscure cases.

1. Select your case. Choose cases in which there are clear divisions and that plainly emphasize the Constitutional issue you wish to teach. If, for example, you wish to highlight the issue of presidential war powers, the *Prize Cases* (1863) or *Youngstown Sheeting and Tubing Co. v. Sawyer* (1952) would be ideal choices. The issue in both cases, the seizure of property by the president in the name of national defense, not only opens up ample opportunity for discourse but forces students to confront Constitutional as well as social, economic, and political considerations of the time.

2. Assign students to the prospective teams. The size of the team depends on your class size. My teams fluctuated between three and six students. Teams including six students can work provided you lay out detailed instructions for the students at the beginning of the trial. On larger teams, assign pairs of students to specific roles relative to the case. In the previous example, for instance, make one pair responsible for looking at the specific language associated with war powers in the Constitution. Have another pair explore precedents the team might use in the case. Have

the final pair be responsible for writing up the document and presenting oral arguments before the class.

3. Engage the evidence. Provide students with carefully edited copies of the case. Make sure the facts of the case are clearly stated. In order to leave students room to do independent research, limit your handout to the edited syllabus of the case along with the facts. Instruct them not to read the Court's decision in the case until after the trial. Give students at least three days to prepare the case, preferably including a weekday so they can meet outside of class to discuss strategy.

4. Begin your mock trial. Have the prosecution put on its case first followed by the defense. Each side should have between 15 and 20 minutes to present its case depending on your class time. Each side should have 5 minutes to present its opening argument, between 12 and 15 minutes to present the main body of its case including witnesses if you are using witnesses and exhibits, and between 3 and 5 minutes for closing statements. Each side should take turns presenting its argument in each phase of the trial. Have the prosecution go first to lay out the issues.

5. Present witness testimony. Many teachers assign students to play the part of witnesses in Court Cases. This can add an extra layer to the case; however, teachers should be very clear in communicating how witnesses are to offer testimony. In the same way that the lawyers are bound by the evidence, so witnesses must respect an acceptable range of responses within the context of the person they are portraying. Limit testimony to one to two witnesses per side. The logic here is twofold. One is to keep your trial on schedule. The other is to allow the prosecution and defense to interact more fully with fewer witnesses rather than rushing through a long list of potentially less significant ones. As your students are building their case you can allow them to identify witnesses they want to call, or you can simply assign witnesses and let both sides know they are available if need be. In the Youngstown case, for example, secretary of commerce Charles Sawyer would be a good witness.

6. Use friend of the court briefs. In reality, witnesses do not testify before the United States Supreme Court but the court will often entertain *amicus curiae* or friend of the court briefs from parties who have an interest in the case. The Court defines it this way: "An amicus curiae brief that brings to the attention of the Court relevant matter not already brought to its attention by the parties may be of considerable help to the Court." In the Youngstown case, for example, the Court heard amicus curiae arguments from the steel workers and rail workers who also would have been impacted by the president's seizure of the mills. If you wish to be faithful to the structure of the Court, you can involve additional students by creating additional teams to address and present amicus curiae briefs before the court to represent these various interests.

7. Assign a jury of one. To assess the students' understanding of the case I generally assigned each student the task of writing an opinion on the case. Generally I advised that the opinions needed to do three basic things. First, they needed to revisit the facts of the case. Second, they needed to present and discuss the issues before the court. Finally, they had to offer a decision in the case and explain their findings relative to the evidence presented during our in-class trial. After students turned in their decisions, I would then share the Court's actual decision with them and entertain questions and a final discussion of the importance of the case and how closely what they found matched up with the justices. Later I began sharing the decision with my students immediately after the trial. I then asked them to take on the role of a newspaper editor writing about the case. In this instance, they needed to do everything outlined above with the added job of explaining how the decision would affect the nation. This allowed students to engage the immediate and long-term results of the decisions of the case we discussed.

Understandably, some teachers have reservations about mock trials because the arguments and results may not mirror those in the actual trial and require an extra layer of explanation that some students might find confusing since they will need to differentiate between the outcome of the mock trial and what happened in real life. This, however, does not mean that they cannot adapt the exercise to address these concerns. One way to ensure historical accuracy is by the teacher taking on the role of the Supreme Court and issuing the final ruling. This, however, may limit the opportunity presented for maximum student participation. Another adaptation is to hold a Moot Court rather than a mock trial. Adopted from the study of the law, in Moot Court students perform a simulation of a hypothetical case before the Supreme Court or other appellate court based on an important constitutional issue. It is a valuable teaching tool for its ability to illustrate to students not only the structure and function of judicial proceedings using important historical content but also the relevance of important court decisions to their own lives. Since the students will be using actual cases that they have read and discussed in class as precedents in their arguments, this method allows them to concentrate on the underlying issues presented in the case rather than the facts of one particular case. A simulated case on Jim Crow segregation, for instance, would allow students to consider the entire body of segregation case law. It also allows students to practice the full range of research, critical thinking, and oral and written communication skills. Moot Court requires a few alterations to the instructions provided for mock trials. First Moot Court exercises should take place after the class has fully discussed the issues and ramifications of the issues associated with the case to ensure that students have a firm grasp of the historical content. Next, the teacher should design a case that engages student interest and presents an opportunity for students to exhibit the full range of knowledge they have acquired relative to the issue at hand.

Historical Figures on Trial

You need not wed your curriculum to actual cases when using SCOTUS. You can put any figure in world history on trial or re-enact with modifications real trials of historical figures. From Louis XVI, Marie Antoinette, and ultimately Robespierre's day of reckoning before revolutionary tribunals in France, to the Terranova trial in Imperial China (see description later in this chapter), to the famous Scopes Monkey trial here in the United States, a fertile playing field of historical content awaits.

Over the years, I have received numerous stories from teachers who applied this method with great success. They demonstrate the creativity and broad range of issues teachers were able to engage using court cases. For instance, an Ohio teacher allowed her students to put Thomas Jefferson on trial for not including women and Blacks in the Declaration of Independence. Her primary documents were selections from Jefferson's Notes on Virginia and the Declaration of Independence. She assigned two four-person teams to prepare cases for the prosecution and for the defense of Jefferson. She then assigned students to play the role of witnesses including George Washington, Phyllis Wheatley, Patrick Henry, Abigail Adams, and Benjamin Banneker. She based her selection of witnesses on documents she assigned each student to read related to their testimony in the case. For the final assessment, she asked the students to write a press release from Jefferson dealing with the allegations and his response to the verdict in the trial.

The Scales of Justice: Weighing the Evidence

A few years ago, while working on an article on the Black Panther Party in Omaha, Nebraska, I came across an interesting account of a trial that took place there in 1971. Two members of the Black Panther Party stood accused of planting a bomb that killed a young police officer. There

were significant questions raised concerning their actual guilt, since most of the evidence against the pair came from a juvenile offender who claimed he had been put up to planting the explosives by the Panthers. Convinced of the Panthers' innocence, former Nebraska governor Frank Morrison took on their case. In his summation before the jury, he had a giant replica of the scales of justice constructed. As he methodically went through the evidence, he placed weights on the scales to indicate those facts that supported his clients' innocence and those which indicated their guilt. When he concluded, the scales tipped prominently in favor of an acquittal.

Although Morrison failed to convince the jury, one way to get middle school students, in particular, to think about the historian's use of evidence is to model Morrison in a fun exercise called the Scales of Justice. First, ask a historically relevant question. Then identify and provide at least six primary and secondary sources related to the question. Present your students with a worksheet with the question written across the top and an image of the scales of justice on it. Ask them to consider the answer to the question in light of each piece of evidence, writing the name of the source or scholarly interpretation in the corresponding scale. After they finish, ask them to write a thesis for an essay and an outline based on how the scales tipped in their consideration of the evidence.

As you are constructing your unit be sure to choose open-ended questions that encourage debate and force them to interrogate each piece of evidence. Examples include:

- Were the Puritans puritanical?
- Was the American Revolution revolutionary?
- Which document freed the slaves, the Emancipation Proclamation or the Thirteenth Amendment?
- In world history, using the example of China consider a "weighing the evidence" exercise on the Opium War.
- If your focus is Europe, consider a question like were "enlightened despots" really enlightened?

Also, try to select interesting historiographical controversies since this will reinforce the notion that scholars are always in dialogue about the past, and as young scholars students are invited to participate in the debate, as long as they are reading and weighing the evidence. I drew the question on the Enlightenment, for instance, from an observation by the great European historian Eugen Webber (1989) who proposed that even as the philosophes celebrated the reforms of so-called enlightened rulers, such as Catherine the Great of Russia, in reality the enlightened despots were always "more despotic than enlightened."

"I Object!" Setting the Rules for Mock Trials

There are really no rules to how you structure the trial; however, I would strongly suggest setting the ground rules for objections. Students' overexposure to countless courtroom dramas left me fielding dozens of objections until I provided my students with some structure. I informed them that they could only object based on the presentation of testimony or facts not in evidence. Defined as those items that your opposition will be willing to concede, I explained to them that facts in evidence, like basic historical facts, are the items upon which all parties can agree. Facts not in evidence, I explained, were observations about the content that were unsubstantiated by the existing documents and evidence.

I was also careful to explain to them the difference between historians and attorneys. Lawyers A. Leo Levin and Robert Levy (1956) have explained that in seeking to persuade, "an advocate may ask the jury to violate all logical rules, and do violence to all the laws of legitimate indifference" (p. 139). In other words, lawyers are free to manipulate the evidence in whatever way best suits their clients. The ultimate measure of their success or failure is their ability to convince a jury of the plausibility of their argument. Thus, while it would probably not be a good idea to argue that aliens abducted a client and programmed him to rob banks, if a lawyer believed that she could convince a jury of this, it would be fair game. Most people, for instance, have heard of the Twinkie defense, where a California barrister was able to convince a jury that his client was guilty of voluntary manslaughter rather than first degree murder due to diminished capacity induced by his consumption of sugary snacks in the weeks leading up to the murders. Historians, I explain to my students, are not advocates, although their interpretations of the past may advocate for a particular viewpoint or position. This would be special pleadings.

A SAMPLING OF COURT CASES

To provide some guidance as to which court cases to explore in history classes, here are three that I have used to engage students.

Murray v. the State of Maryland

The case of Donald Murray versus the State of Maryland from 1936 (Raymond A. Pearson v. Donald G. Murray, 1936) had all of the elements I needed to teach both content and critical thinking skills. It was one of Thurgood Marshall's first segregation cases in the efforts of the National Association for the Advancement of Colored People (NAACP) to dismantle the precedent established by the Supreme Court in *Plessy v. Ferguson* (1896). It was also an ideal case because of the numerous problems associated with the type of argument Marshall, and now my students, needed to make. I divided the class up into six legal teams of four and presented an imaginary scenario to them.

I circumvented the old standby of students looking up the case by telling them that I would be evaluating the teams on the merits of their arguments. I further warned them that there was no guarantee that I would decide in the same manner as had the Maryland Supreme Court.

Filling the Shoes of Thurgood Marshall

Much like Thurgood Marshall before him, Donald Murray longed to attend the University of Maryland Law School. Barred from applying due to a state segregation ordinance requiring separate facilities for those of the white and colored races, Murray decided to sue the state of Maryland. Since Maryland did not have a law school for "colored" people, Murray reasoned that he was denied his rights under the Fourteenth Amendment to the Constitution. As his attorney, he secured Marshall, a recent graduate of Howard University in Washington DC and a lawyer for the NAACP. In an effort to placate Murray, the state offered him a deal. Maryland would pay tuition for him to attend any university in the nation that would accept him and provide a small stipend for living expenses. Marshall, however, convinced Murray that his suit was winnable if the NAACP asked the right questions. He saw a chink in Maryland's segregation ordinance rooted not only in the language of the Fourteenth Amendment but also in the failure of Maryland's deal to meet the full requirements of the Supreme Court's *Plessy v. Ferguson* doctrine of separate but equal.

What issues did Marshall intend to present before the court? Unfortunately, no one knows. He scheduled a briefing with junior counsel working on the case to share his ideas for 10:30 this morning. Last evening, however, his wife rushed him to the hospital after he fell ill. This phantom illness has left him unable to communicate. This morning Marshall's former Dean and mentor and the head of the NAACP Legal Defense Fund, Charles Hamilton Houston, has called you into his office. He has asked that you make the oral arguments before the Maryland Supreme Court in Marshall's place. Marshall left a satchel filled with documents on his desk in preparation for the briefing. Inside was a well marked-up copy of Justice Brown's majority opinion in *Plessy v. Ferguson*, a worn copy of John Marshall Harlan's dissent from the same case, a crisp copy of the Fourteenth Amendment, several brochures from law schools around the country, and a copy of the requirements to pass the Maryland bar exam. "We hope Thurgood can recover in time," Houston explains as he hands you the satchel, "but right now you are the only hope. You have three days to prepare your argument. As always, my door is open, but we are all counting on you."

In contrast to the other cases, in this scenario all six teams were working for Murray. I told the students that I would represent the state of Maryland. I handed the assignment out on a Monday and told the students we would discuss the case on Friday. Each team would have an opportunity to present its case for five minutes, with me recording a basic outline of their arguments on the board. I then would respond to their arguments as the state of Maryland before allowing each team a three to four minute rebuttal and final statement. I at this point had switched hats and would be making my decision as the presiding judge in the case.

In stark contrast to the failed brief exercise, the class was literally abuzz with activity over the next few days. Bombarded with student questions and yet again chastised by the librarian for not giving her proper notice that my students would be doing a research project that would require them to access law journals, the in-class discussion was amazing. What I assumed would take about 35 minutes consumed the entire period as my students debated the merits not only of the case but also of each other's arguments. During debrief several students explained how they were reticent about the case being presented by their team, but had gone along or argued vigorously for their position as they were preparing their arguments. I took this opportunity to give them examples of how defense teams often disagree, arguing over approaches and the presentation of evidence, although you rarely see that in the final defense. This is the same with historians, I explained. They wrestle with the evidence behind the scenes. What you read in your textbook is a synthesis of the collected works of historians, but this does not mean that there is 100% agreement. History is constantly being rewritten and debated.

In retrospect, one of the reasons the exercise worked so well was because it allowed my students to confront a series of emerging problems in pursuit of the goal of having Murray admitted to the law school. As Jean Piaget, the renowned scholar of child development, proposed:

> Real comprehension of a notion or a theory implies the reinvention of this theory by the student. Once the child is capable of repeating certain notions and using some applications of these in learning situations, he gives the impression of understanding: however, this does not fulfill the condition of reinvention. True understanding manifests itself by new spontaneous applications (quoted in Wiggins & McTighe, 1998, p. 94).

The spontaneous applications of my students came during the trial. As the students presented their cases, they were forced to contend with the arguments and evidence offered by the opposition. Limited by the evidence and witness testimony, as the case took new turns and directions, they had to adapt, revisit, and reexamine their understanding of the Fourteenth Amendment and their legal strategies. I never got tired of the late afternoon or early morning visits from student attorneys eager to share their discovery of new evidence or new arguments. They were applying what they learned in ways that far exceeded my wildest expectations. It also provided me with the opportunity to really engage them, not merely as an instructor but, consistent with the work of Theodore Sizer (1992), more as a coach. I found myself guiding them more by asking questions and making suggestions than supplying answers. They rewarded my patience by finding the very evidence and making the same arguments I would have covered in class. The difference, of course, was the excitement and intellectual growth they experienced in the process of discovery. Learning was no longer limited to exchanges in the classroom. During the trial, we always seemed to be in running dialogue about the case and by extension history and the meaning of important concepts related to civic participation and citizenship.

Buchanan v. Warley

One of my favorite cases was the residential segregation case *Buchanan v. Warley* from 1917. It involved the following Louisville, Kentucky, segregation law:

> An ordinance to prevent conflict and ill feeling between the white and colored races in the City of Louisville, and to preserve the public peace and promote the general welfare by making reasonable provisions requiring, as far as practicable, the use of separate blocks for residences, places of abode and places of assembly by white and colored people respectively.

Representing the plaintiff was the newly formed NAACP. In order to understand how and what the association would argue, students selected to argue for the Association had to answer the following questions, along with weighing the evidence and building their case:

- What is the NAACP?
- When was it founded?
- Why would the organization be interested in this case?
- When did residential segregation begin? Had it ever been challenged in court before?
- Do you recognize any crossovers, comparisons, and connections with other events we have studied?
- If you were arguing against the Kentucky Law, what would be the Core of your argument?

Students that were representing the state had to answer the following:

- What is residential segregation?
- When did the practice begin?
- Why is the Kentucky law worded in the way that it is?
- Do you recognize any crossovers, comparisons, and connections with other events we have studied?

Interestingly enough, although the impulse toward residential segregation was evident in the various Black Codes that emerged after the Civil War, the first city to pass a city ordinance was Baltimore, Maryland, in 1910. States adopting residential segregation laws argued for their legality under the precedent established by the Supreme Court in the

Slaughterhouse Cases (1873). In those cases, dealing with pollution caused by butchers, the Court ruled that it fell under the logical exercise of the police powers of the state to deal with matters of public safety, such as public health, within its own borders. With the double-digit lynching and contested-area riots that swept the nation after the turn of the century, Baltimore and later Louisville's ordinances seemed reasonable. Many states adopted residential segregation ordinances, claiming as Kentucky did that the purpose of the act was to preserve peace and good order among the races. Arguing on behalf of the state, students would have to engage issues with clear crossovers to their lives in the present day, thus enriching the exercise.

The Case of Francis Terranova

In the summer of 1995, I found myself struggling to come up with activities for active learning for a course in Chinese history. Part of my course load at the high school was to teach the history of China to ninth graders. Surrounded by stacks of books from the library and three binders full of resources left by my predecessor, I was nevertheless troubled. How was I, so far removed from my area of expertise, going to make the course interesting, challenging, and fun? I was stuck until I read about the case of an Italian sailor, Francis Terranova, who was tried in Canton, China, in 1821.

Justice in Canton

Italian sailor Francis Terranova was working aboard an American vessel in the British-controlled port of Canton when Chinese authorities demanded that he be turned over to them for trial for his alleged involvement in the death of a local merchant woman. The woman, Ko Leang, was one of many merchants who filled the harbor in hopes of exchanging goods with the westerners in the tightly controlled port. On the morning of her death, Leang pulled her tiny junk alongside the soaring American trading vessel, the *Emily*, on which Terranova worked. Witnesses reported hearing a heated exchange between the sailor and the vendor and later seeing Terranova discard an earthenware pot overboard. It struck the woman on the head and sent her tumbling into the sea where she drowned.

Positively identified by the onlookers, Terranova bitterly protested his innocence, pleading with his superiors to protect him. At first the captain of the *Emily* defied demands by the Manchu government to turn over the frightened sailor to authorities. No doubt mindful of previous instances in which western sailors were made to pay steep penalties, including the death penalty, for transgressing the laws of China, he resolved to insure Terranova's safety. However, when Chinese authorities threatened to suspend all American trade in the harbor, an order that could possibly have led to the

Chinese confiscating the cargo of ships already in port, the captain was forced to reconsider. Rumors abounded that the *Emily*, like many other western trading vessels, was carrying large quantities of opium, an illegal narcotic forbidden for importation by the Chinese. Concerned that a failure to relinquish Terranova might result in even more trouble, the captain relented and released the sailor into the custody of Chinese authorities. After a hasty trial, with westerners barred from giving testimony, Terranova received the death penalty. He was executed by strangulation the following day (Donahue, 1982; Spence, 1999; Williams, 1922).

The facts of the case had all the hallmarks of a good mystery. I pondered how I might adapt it for use with the ninth-grade students. I started to think about the questions it raised:

- Who was Francis Terranova?
- How did he come to serve aboard an American vessel?
- Who was Ko Leang?
- Why was she selling fruit in Canton harbor?
- Why did the British control the port of Canton?

These were all questions that I could creatively lead my students to ask if I could somehow convince them, as Terranova's newly constituted legal defense team, that they would be responsible for making a case before the Manchu authorities in Canton to spare his life.

I assigned two legal teams, one Anglo-American team to defend Terranova and one Chinese team to argue for his just punishment. I also assigned several students to special roles including the captain of the *Emily*, Lo Keang's husband, a representative of the British East India Company, a Manchu official charged with policing the port of Canton, and of course Terranova. I provided each person with one primary source and a few lines on their character. They were responsible for researching the rest. For the representative of the British East India Company, for instance, I assigned a few pages that I provided from E. M. Gull's *British Economic Interests in the Far East* (1943). Gull quotes an East India official who succinctly summarized the company's position prior to the Opium War as follows: "We are bound to submit to your laws while we are in your waters; be they ever so unjust, we will not resist them" (p. 18). Noting that his letter came well after the Terranova case, I instructed the Manchu official to read it to get a sense of how a British official might respond.

For evidence, I gave all the students four documents detailing the onset of problems between China and Great Britain on the eve of the Terranova trial.

Document One

The Reception of the First English Ambassador Lord Macartney to China (1792)
(Tappan, 1914, pp. 189–192)

Document Two

Ch'ien Lung's Edict to King George III of England (1793)
(Craig, 2001, pp. 133)

Document Three

Commissioner Chin urges Morality on Queen Victoria (1839)
(Craig, 2001, p. 126)

Document Four

The People of Canton: Against the English (1842)
(Tappan, 1914, p. 197)

I wanted them to understand the deep social and cultural issues that divided China and the West in the decades leading up to not only Terranova's execution but also the Opium Wars (1839–1842) and the signing of the Treaty of Nanking (1842)—what Chinese critics consistently referred to as the "unequal treaties" that forever changed China. I wanted the students to see that this was a two-way street and that in the Intersection of international relations, both sides made mistakes.

One document I gave them was the full text of the Emperor Qialong's letter to King George III from 1793 denying Great Britain's request to open up new avenues of trade. In the letter, the emperor boldly declared:

> As your Ambassador can see for himself, we possess all things. I set no value on objects strange or ingenious, and have no use for your country's manufactures. This then is my answer to your request to appoint a representative at my Court, a request contrary to our dynastic usage, which would only result in inconvenience to yourself. I have expounded my wishes in detail and have commanded your tribute Envoys to leave in peace on their homeward journey. It behooves you, O King, to respect my sentiments and to display even greater devotion and loyalty in future, so that, by perpetual submission to our Throne, you may secure peace and prosperity for your country hereafter. (Backhouse & Bland, 1914, pp. 322–331)

I also gave them a heavily edited passage from Joshua Gee's 1730 publication on English mercantilism. In it, Gee expounded on the necessities of

British mercantilism, with an emphasis on the need to maintain a favorable balance of trade. Although the other documents came after the trial of Terranova, I shared them with the students as part of building a complete portrait of escalating tensions between the British and the Manchu dynasty.

The trial turned out to be a great success. The students really enjoyed it, but more important, it really opened them up to the significance of trying to appreciate cultural perspectives. I had also given them the opportunity to exhibit what they had learned through the course of the trial. As the final assessment, I asked each student to write a decision in the case based on Chinese law and the evidence in the case.

QUESTIONS FOR REVIEW AND REFLECTION

1. After reading the chapter, what important court cases that you currently teach might be adaptable as SCOTUS exercises or mock trials? Based on the information in the chapter and in the resources section, spend a few moments thinking about how you might structure such a trial.

2. Survey your state content standards for court cases. Are there any likely candidates for inclusion in your course as a mock trial exercises? Take a look at the resources and further reading section of this chapter. What additional resources might you need to prepare a mock trial on the cases in your standards?

3. Guest speakers and outside guests often bring out the best in students. Are there any legal professionals, including attorneys, police officers, professors, or judges that you can invite to your class to observe or perhaps participate in this exercise with your students?

4. Team teaching can yield wonderful results under certain circumstances. Are there other history teachers in your school or district who would be willing to conduct a joint SCOTUS exercise with you and your class?

5. Teachers take different approaches in creating their SCOTUS characters. Some use the names and images of actual jurists like John Marshall, Thurgood Marshall, or Sandra Day O'Connor. Others create their own characters or invite student input. Assuming that you plan to make SCOTUS a regular part of curriculum, how might you design your character?

REFERENCES

Backhouse, E. and Bland, J. O. P. (1914). *Annals and memoirs of the court of Peking*. Boston: Houghton Mifflin.
Buchanan v. Warley, 245 U.S. 60 (1917).
Craig, A. (2001). *The heritage of Chinese civilization*. Englewood Cliffs, NJ: Prentice Hall.
Donahue, W. J. (1981). The Francis Terranova case. *The Historian, 43*, 211–224.
Raymond A. Pearson v. Donald G. Murray, 169 Md. 478 (1936).

Gull, E. M. (1943). *British economic interests in the Far East.* New York: Institute of Pacific Relations.

Levin, A. L. & Levy, R. J. (1956). Persuading the jury with facts not in evidence: The fiction–science spectrum. *University of Pennsylvania Law Review, 105(2),* 139–184.

Plessy v. Ferguson, 163 U.S. 537 (1896). Retrieved March 24, 2008, from http://www.oyez .org/cases/1851–1900/1895/1895_210/

Prize Cases, 67 U.S. 635 (1863). Retrieved March 24, 2008, from http://www.oyez.org/ cases/1851–1900/1862/1862_0/

Slaughterhouse Cases, 83 U.S. 36 (1873). Retrieved March 24, 2008, from http://www.oyez .org/cases/1851–1900/1872/1872_2/

Sizer, T.R. (1992). *Horace's school: Redesigning the American high school.* Boston: Houghton Mifflin.

Spence, J. D. (1999). *The search for modern China.* New York: Norton.

Tappan, E. M. (Ed.). (1914). *The world's story: A history of the world in story, song, and art: Vol. 1. China, Japan, and the islands of the Pacific.* Boston: Houghton Mifflin.

Webber, E. (1989). *The Western tradition: Vol. 35. The Enlightenment* [Video recording]. Boston: WGBH Boston.

Wiggins, G. & McTighe, J. (1998). *Understanding by design.* Alexandria, VA: Association for Supervision and Curriculum Development.

Williams, B. H. (1922). The protection of American citizens in China: Extraterritoriality. *The American Journal of International Law, 16(1),* 43–58.

RESOURCES AND FURTHER READING

Dorf, M. (Ed.). (2004). *Constitutional law stories.* New York: Foundation Press.

Edited by law professor Michael Dorf, this incredibly rich volume explores 15 landmark cases by examining the intriguing stories behind each case from *Maurbury v. Madison* to *Clinton v. Jones.* This is a must-have resource if you are considering making court cases a regular part of your curriculum.

Downs, J. M. (2003). The fateful case of Francis Terranova: An incident of the China trade. *Mains'l Haul: A Journal of Pacific Maritime History, 39(2),* 4–13

This article is a good source of information on the Terranova trial.

Foley, G. (2007). The *Prize Cases* and Lincoln's Supreme Court. *Lincoln Herald, 109,* 83–101.

This very accessible article on the *Prize Cases* of 1863 provides an excellent overview of the circumstances leading to one of the Supreme Court's most significant rulings regarding presidential war powers. This is another great court case to explore with your students.

Lubet, S. (2004). *Murder in Tombstone: The forgotten trial of Wyatt Earp.* New Haven: Yale University Press

This is a good book for those interested in creating a trial on the Wild West engaging the life of one of the most colorful historical characters of the period.

Orser, E. (1997). Neither separate nor equal: Foreshadowing Brown in Baltimore County, 1935–1937. *Maryland Historical Magazine, 92(1),* 4–35.

An outstanding student-friendly account of Thurgood Marshall's early desegregation efforts in Baltimore, this would be an ideal place to start for those interested in adapting the case involving Marshall, Murray v. Maryland, presented in this chapter.

Russell, F. (1975). Sacco and Vanzetti: Was the trial fair? *Modern Age, 19(1),* 30–41.

This is a solid treatment of the Sacco and Vanzetti case. While there are sources that are more recent and abundant materials on the Web, this is still a good place to begin designing a mock trial on this case.

Tushnet, M. V. (1997). *Making Constitutional law: Thurgood Marshall and the Supreme Court, 1961–1991*. New York: Oxford University Press.

A good source for building teacher content knowledge on Thurgood Marshall, this book also discusses many of the cases Marshall was involved in as a justice on the Court, making it a great place to look for potential subjects for cases as well.

Wiecek, W. M. (1978). Slavery and abolition before the United States Supreme Court, 1820–1860. *Journal of American History, 65(1),* 34–59.

A wonderfully succinct essay outlining several important cases dealing with slavery and abolition that were heard by the Marshall and Taney Courts between the Missouri Compromise and the onset of the Civil War, this is a great place to start if the antebellum period is a major part of your curriculum.

Waley, A. (1958). *The Opium War through Chinese eyes*. London: George Allen & Unwin.

This is a good resource on Anglo Chinese relations, especially for teachers interested in building content knowledge and creating a trial based on this most interesting chapter in U.S. and world history.

Wolcott, L. (1991). Their day in court. Students learn about America's legal system by taking part in it. *Teacher Magazine, 2,* 24–29.

This article discusses the use of mock trials and other legal based activities by teachers in a number of elementary and junior high schools. The author notes how student participation in these types of activities can provide a rewarding experience for students and shares statistics on their effectiveness as a teaching tool.

ON THE WEB

Landmark Supreme Court cases. (n.d.). Retrieved March 20, 2008, from http://www .landmarkcases.org/

Although limited in the number of actual cases available, this site has a wealth of resources related to using court cases in class, including an excellent section devoted to conducting mock trials and moot court activities in your classroom, complete with detailed instructions on how to structure your trial. This site is highly recommended for middle school and high school teachers looking to incorporate elements of legal contests into their teaching.

Oyez: Tour. (n.d.). Retrieved March 20, 2008, from http://www.oyez.org/tour/

With an extensive database of state court and United States Supreme Court cases, this highly navigable Web site is an outstanding resource for building content knowledge for SCOTUS activities in your classroom. While the site is not as teacher friendly as landmarkcases.org, it is well worth the time in terms of identifying cases and gathering background information for your cases.

6

ESP+C

Providing a Student Mental
Organizer and Writing Strategy

*Historical thinking, like other forms of disciplinary thinking, begins
with clear-eyed wonder before the world.*

—Lendol Calder

When I started teaching high school, I realized just how pervasive a
problem organizing and writing information was for some of my
students. Even something as simple as writing a thesis statement to begin
an essay seemed to confound them. Despite my frustration at times, I tried
to be patient. I constantly reminded myself of my own struggles with math
as a child—how I did the long slow burn every time someone would declare
math easy as I struggled to make Cs. That is, until I discovered formulas.
By the time we started algebra and geometry, my grades improved ever so
slightly, mainly because one could at least earn partial credit for knowing
the formulas. I made it a point to know the formulas. As I worked through
writing issues with my ninth and eleventh graders, I came to appreciate the
need to present historical writing to some degree as a formula. While some
would bristle at the thought that anything related to the humanities could

be reduced to a formula, in fact good writing, like good art and good music, makes use of formulas. These do not necessarily rob the artists or the writer of their creativity as much as creating a familiar format for their audience. ESP+C—standing for Economic, Social, Political, plus Cultural—was my attempt to create such a formula for history and social studies students.

WHAT IS ESP+C?

A sampling of state content standards reveals that nearly all ask students to evaluate historical phenomena in terms of four factors: economic, social, political, and cultural. This is not to say that other considerations are not important. Content standards also often refer to factors like religion and geography, but ESP+C are by far the most common.

While the economic, social, and political are obvious, and I described my use of ESP in Chapter 1, I would spend some time talking to my students about the importance of *culture* in understanding the past. My views on culture developed largely out of my reading of the great English historian E. P. Thompson (1991), who emphasizes that culture was a product of conflict. The cultural world exposed by Thompson is very much a place of Intersections, murky, grimy, riddled with contradictions, but also very dynamic and full of life. In order to get my students to appreciate the importance of culture, I told them that the C in my formula was silent. However, to leave it out, like forgetting to include a silent letter in a word, could radically change the meaning of an episode or event in history. Thus, when using ESP, they always had to remember to relate the importance of culture and how it is influenced by history.

I sold my students on the use of ESP+C as their magic crystal ball into history. As with many of my other strategies, ESP+C included a few tantalizing features drawn from popular culture. At the time, the hottest program on television was the *X-Files,* a show about an unconventional FBI agent Fox Mulder and his by-the-book partner Dana Scully. Mulder, whose nickname was Agent Spooky, was always looking for explanations outside the realm of reality. Also on TV were these bad commercials for a purported psychic named Mrs. Cleo. For 99 cents a minute, plus tax, Cleo pledged to put you in contact with lost loved ones. In addition, many of my students were devotees first of *Buffy the Vampire Slayer* and much later of the *Harry Potter* book series so there was a natural tie-in and interest. ESP+C was born.

Many psychic investigators profess the ability to obtain information by paranormal means independent of any known physical senses or deduction from previous experience. Historians too claim to know about the past. Although their knowledge comes from more conventional methods, including the collection and deciphering of evidence, the information they produce is nonetheless a portal to worlds gone by. From political systems, to social customs, to forms of economic exchange and cultural practices, historians bring the past alive and allow us to communicate with historical figures long gone.

The novelty of ESP+C disguises its ability to help the students who may not be the strongest in history have at least a fighting chance to understand the most basic concepts associated with its study. We cannot equip our students with a magic wand, like Harry Potter, so that they can simply zap the right answer. We can offer them a type of magical crystal ball, ESP+C, which gives them a basic outline of what to look for when researching or writing about history. ESP+C has three levels as a method of analysis, a mental organizer, and a writing tool. Each can contribute to student understanding and engagement with history.

The Three Types of Historical ESP

Often referred to as the sixth sense, there are many different types of ESP in the world of science fiction and parapsychology. Three approximate some of the work we do as historians. They are remote viewing, precognition, and telepathy. Parapsychologists maintain that remote viewing is the ability to see people, places, or events from a distance by means other than the normal senses. Precognition, on the other hand, refers to the belief that psychics can see things before they happen and foretell the future. Finally, there is telepathy. Telepaths profess the ability to communicate with others through the power of the mind, even beyond the grave. While these seem to have little to do with history at first blush, how you present them to your students can open up a world of opportunity.

Remote Viewing

First, historical scholarship is by definition about remote viewing. Far removed not only by time, but also in many instances by place from the events they are studying, historians already practice a form of remote viewing. Even when historians are able to handle the actual materials from a period in a library or archives, they are viewing these from a distance, both in time and space. In studying local history, for instance, it is always fascinating to read about events that occurred in a place where the buildings and other reference points no longer exist. To reconstruct the past the historian must be able to see what was in order to paint an accurate portrait of that particular historical moment.

Distance is a critical part of history in that in order to be "objective," historians must have a degree of separation from their subjects. Remote viewing corresponds with the following of the Bradley Commission's (1989) habits of the mind (see the full list in the Introduction):

2. Distinguish between the important and the inconsequential, to develop the "discriminating memory" needed for a discerning judgment in public and personal life.

6. Comprehend the interplay of change and continuity, and avoid assuming that either is somehow more natural, or more to be expected, than the other.

7. Prepare to live with uncertainties and exasperating, even perilous, unfinished business, realizing that not all problems have solutions.

8. Grasp the complexity of historical causation, respect particularity, and avoid excessively abstract generalizations.

12. Understand the relationship between geography and history as a matrix of time and place, and as context for events.

Precognition

The second application of ESP is precognition, the ability to know the future before it happens. I use it conversely as a tool to encourage students to hypothesize about the past based on what they already know. The Bradley Commission's habits of mind that most closely related to precognition exercises appear below:

7. Prepare to live with uncertainties and exasperating, even perilous, unfinished business, realizing that not all problems have solutions.

8. Grasp the complexity of historical causation, respect particularity, and avoid excessively abstract generalizations.

9. Appreciate the often tentative nature of judgments about the past, and thereby avoid the temptation to seize upon particular "lessons" of history as cures for present ills.

Telepathy

Finally, telepathy involves the researcher or historian critically reading the sources and communicating with other historians in search of an explanation of the past. The Bradley Commission's habits of mind that are related to telepathy are as follows:

1. Understand the significance of the past to their own lives, both private and public, and to their society.

3. Perceive past events and issues as they were experienced by people at the time, to develop historical empathy as opposed to present-mindedness.

4. Acquire at one and the same time a comprehension of diverse cultures and of shared humanity.

Many teachers already encourage student participation in activities that rely on a form of "history telepathy"—in reality anticipatory thinking. For instance, in the popular Brown Bear exercise, which many middle school teachers use, as the students trade names of historical persons or events, they are dialoguing about history. Teachers also ask students to write letters to people who have gone before or create dialogue between historical actors, exercises that can be classified as a form of "historical telepathy." Introducing students to the idea of telepathy is one way to remind them what the overarching point of these exercises is—to think critically about and develop a sense of historical empathy with those in the past in a way that is fun and exciting. A number of teachers, for instance, already employ the Spirit Reading or Jump-in Reading exercise as a class reading activity. With its three layers, ESP makes a nice addition to this. The idea here again is to take something that is really fun and interesting to students and to tie it to the study of history.

ESP+C as a Mental Organizer

By encouraging our students to use ESP+C, we can equip them with a basic framework for processing and organizing information as well as understanding how, in much simplified terms, the historian works. Two of the most popular approaches to thematic-based history instruction are the diachronic and synchronic approaches.

- The *diachronic approach* takes a theme, such as war, technology, or ideas about government like absolutism, and examines its impact on history from one period or date to another. Commonly anchored by watershed events, one might trace the rise of nationalism, from the American and French Revolutions to German Unification in the 1870s.
- The *synchronic approach* traces several themes over time. Using the same period from above, you would ask students to examine the forces of liberalism and nationalism. As Fred Drake and Lynn Nelson (2004) observe, the "synchronic approach considers the relationship of multiple political, economic, and social phenomena within a short period of time" (p. 83).

Used in conjunction with both approaches, ESP+C can help students appreciate historical relationships more deeply by providing them with four basic factors that they should always be looking to assess. In the case of a diachronic examination of a war, for example, students using ESP+C would know to look for the war's causes and impacts in these four critical areas. For natural disasters, they would be looking to evaluate the impact on the politics, economics, societal relations, and culture of various communities over time, say from the Johnstown flood that ravaged Pennsylvania in 1889 to Hurricane Katrina and its impact on New Orleans in 2005.

The same would be true of the synchronic approach. Asked to assess the impact of liberalism and nationalism from 1789 to 1880, students would use their ESP+C to tease out the impact of these two important political ideologies on the politics, economics, social relations, and culture of Western Europe and the Americas.

This not to say that there are not other significant factors, but ESP+C provides a simple means for students to recall what is most important. The point is to keep it simple. The more unwieldy or unrelated the tool, the more difficult it is for students to remember and use. Furthermore, many of the additions that one might include, such as science and religion, are themselves themes and could be subsumed under the four broad categories already established. While this does not address the concern of geography, the fact that both approaches look at phenomena over time and space means that students, by definition, will need to engage geography. For example, the changing of national boundaries occasioned by the "blood and iron" chancellor Otto Von Bismarck's unification of Germany changed the political geography of Western Europe. Again, one of the more attractive features of ESP+C is its simplicity and ease of application for students. ESP+C becomes a mental organizer for students, enabling them to work systematically to explain any given period, regardless of time or place, and making clear what important points to take away.

USING ESP+C

ESP+C can be used in many different ways to enhance instruction. I have included several approaches here along with examples of how I implemented this strategy.

The first way to use ESP+C is as a mental organizer. For this approach I typically would use ESP+C in conjunction with exercises that have steps that engage prior knowledge such as Directed Reading or Directed Listening Activities (Stauffer, 1975). In addition to setting the exercise up as a form of remote viewing, I modified the standard Directed Reading/Listening Activity by adding a step using ESP+C. In the standard approach, for example, the teacher will hold up an image or read the title of a text and ask students to make predictions of what the reading will be about simply based on the title or image. My exercise began the same way. However after the students identified what they knew, I would then ask them to use ESP+C to review the same image or title. In addition to being able to identify familiar words or images, I would ask them to engage the economic, social, political, and cultural significance of the words and images they identified in relation to any recognizable dates. Take the political cartoon from the St. Louis *Republic* that appears at the end of this chapter, for instance (Figure 6.3). If your students were able to identify the picture as a woman sitting between a donkey and an elephant, you could further engage them using ESP by asking questions about the meaning of those images, like, Where have we seen those animal representations before and what did they mean? What do you think the author was trying to convey about the woman in politics based on this? Since the year 1920 is visible in the cartoon, you could further ask the students to consider the significance of the year in their analysis of the image.

The rest of the exercise follows the standard approach. Here it is completely mapped out.

An ESP+C Directed Reading–Directed Listening Activity

1. The teacher shares a cartoon, image, book cover, or title of a book or article with the class. With this limited amount of information the teacher asks the class to make predictions about what they think the reading will be about. Again using Figure 6.3 as an example the teacher might ask, "What do you think this cartoon is about? Explain." The teacher should have a scribe record a list of all the things the students are able to tease out concerning the image or title based on their prior knowledge. (Try to select titles, images, or photographs that include dates. This, I have found, provides students with important markers that help stimulate thinking and also channel their thinking toward the time period under consideration.)

2. After the students have exhausted their prior knowledge, the teacher should ask them to perform the same task, this time applying ESP+C. The teacher has two options here: either ask students to start from scratch viewing the cartoon all over again with their ESP+C filters on or simply have them ESP+C the list they were able to come up with from Step 1. (If you were using a text like John Wesley Hardin's autobiography, discussed in Chapter 2, you could do the same thing by asking students to reflect on the ESP+C of the title and dates provided by Brown in his title.)

3. At this point, based on Step 1 and Step 2 the teacher asks the students to make predictions about what they think the cartoonist was attempting to convey or what the reading is about. The scribe should record these, along with the students' rationale for each prediction. As in the standard exercise, this allows students to activate prior knowledge and gain important background information before reading the text.

4. The teacher instructs students either as a class or in groups to read the text up to a predetermined stop. At this point, the teacher asks the students to revisit their previous predictions and asks if they would like to make new ones based on the new evidence. The class repeats this until they have completed the text.

5. Once they have finished reading, the teacher should have the students review their predictions with an eye toward uncovering what clues and information proved useful; what proved to be misleading or confusing; and what they uncovered that was surprising, unusual, or unexpected.

Another way to use ESP+C is through a form of historical telepathy using documents. The purpose here is to have students try to foresee the course of action of a historical figure based on their reading and understanding of that person's previous writings, expressions, and or actions. What you want to do here is

1. Identify an important intersection in history where a historical actor has had to make a difficult decision or choose a course of action. Find two primary sources in close chronological proximity to one another written by or about that figure that illustrate her or his views or objectives. Provide students with the first document in chronological order.

2. Have the students either individually or as a class read and review the document using their ESP+C filters. Have them map out the major ideas, views, values, and/or philosophies of the person being considered.

3. Introduce the historical dilemma, opportunity, or problem that has presented itself and ask the students, based on the knowledge they have gained of the individual under consideration, to write a speech or decide a course of action for the individual.

4. Have the students prepare a written assignment, either a speech or a paper outlining what they think that person would do or say. In class have the students share their ideas and debate which comes closest to the spirit and letter of the original document and the ideas and philosophies of its principle.

5. Once the students have had an opportunity to fully discuss the issues, share with them the second document by the historical figure that represents a resolution of the problem or a further statement on the issues they were asked to consider. Once again have the students review their predictions with an eye toward uncovering what clues and information proved useful; what proved to be misleading or confusing; and what they uncovered that was surprising, unusual, or unexpected.

6. For homework have students do a short writing assignment based on what they learned about this individual using ESP+ C.

Here is a detailed example of this approach using actual documents.

Martin Luther King Jr. in the Intersection

Background: In April of 1963 Martin Luther King Jr. found himself at a crossroads. In jail in Birmingham, Alabama, for contempt of court and parading without a permit, King wrote his response in the margins of the New York Times. Four months later he would have an opportunity to share his views with the entire nation. What would he say?

1. Provide students with a primary or secondary source on a topic in history. The two documents that I most often used with the Civil Rights era were the Reverend Dr. Martin Luther King Jr.'s letter from a

Birmingham jail, published on April 16, 1963 (see the text reproduced in the next section), and his "I have a dream" speech, delivered four months later on August 28 in Washington DC.

2. Have the students read and discuss the first document. In examining Dr. King's letter from a Birmingham jail, I first asked students to SOAP and Fingerprint it (see Chapter 3). When they finished, I would give them a little more background on the movement up until the March on Washington.

3. Ask the students to perform a bit of mental telepathy. Using my example, I would ask what Dr. King would say in his "I Have a Dream" speech, based on their understanding of the movement and his earlier writing from Birmingham jail. Specifically I asked them to consider how King might answer his critics, inspire his supporters, and convince those on the light of caution that his course was the right one. Along with this, I asked if, given his audience, King's content and tone would be different from his letter and if he might discuss ideas similar to those he expressed in Birmingham. For homework, I asked them to "channel" Dr. King's spirit and write his speech for the March on Washington. To discourage students from simply looking up King's speech, I would explain to them beforehand that I would not be grading them solely on how close they came to King's actual words at the March on Washington, but on how much their speeches captured the spirit of King's letter from the Birmingham jail. I would expect them to return to many of the issues raised by King in Birmingham but put on a national stage in Washington DC.

4. The next day we would read, compare, and discuss their speeches. Toward the end of class, I would provide them with a printed copy of the speech and also play a video recording of King's speech in class. For the next day's homework, I would ask them to review King's speech and assess how close they came to King's words and ideas in their speeches. As a final assessment I asked them to write a final reflection paper identifying the economic, social, and political underpinnings of King's message in the letter from a Birmingham jail and his "I have a dream" speech. I also asked them to discuss at least two ways in which the goals and values expressed by King continue to shape American culture.

A SAMPLING OF ESP+C

Analyzing King's Letter From a Birmingham Jail

Here is an example of using ESP+C as a writing tool using the same primary source mentioned above—Dr. King's letter from a Birmingham jail—to help students identify and organize information. A teacher could introduce the lesson as follows:

In his letter from a Birmingham jail, Dr. King highlighted various forms of discrimination visited upon people of color that would not allow him to yield to the demands of the Birmingham clergy to leave the city. Here is an excerpt from his letter. Using the ESP+C strategy, identify the economic, social, political, and cultural examples he provides of inequality directed against African Americans in Birmingham.

"Why We Can't Wait"

We have waited for more than 340 years for our constitutional and God-given rights. The nations of Asia and Africa are moving with jetlike speed toward gaining political independence, but we still creep at horse-and-buggy pace toward gaining a cup of coffee at a lunch counter. Perhaps it is easy for those who have never felt the stinging dark of segregation to say, "Wait." But when you have seen vicious mobs lynch your mothers and fathers at will and drown your sisters and brothers at whim; when you have seen hate-filled policemen curse, kick and even kill your black brothers and sisters; when you see the vast majority of your twenty million Negro brothers smothering in an airtight cage of poverty in the midst of an affluent society; when you suddenly find your tongue twisted and your speech stammering as you seek to explain to your six-year-old daughter why she can't go to the public amusement park that has just been advertised on television, and see tears welling up in her eyes when she is told that Funtown is closed to colored children, and see ominous clouds of inferiority beginning to form in her little mental sky, and see her beginning to distort her personality by developing an unconscious bitterness toward white people; when you have to concoct an answer for a five-year-old son who is asking: "Daddy, why do white people treat colored people so mean?"; when you take a cross-county drive and find it necessary to sleep night after night in the uncomfortable corners of your automobile because no motel will accept you; when you are humiliated day in and day out by nagging signs reading "white" and "colored"; when your first name becomes "nigger," your middle name becomes "boy" (however old you are) and your last name becomes "John," and your wife and mother are never given the respected title "Mrs."; when you are harried by day and haunted by night by the fact that you are a Negro, living constantly at tiptoe stance, never quite knowing what to expect next, and are plagued with inner fears and outer resentments; when you are forever fighting a degenerating sense of "nobodiness" then you will understand why we find it difficult to wait. There comes a time when the cup of endurance runs over, and men are no longer willing to be plunged into the abyss of despair. I hope, sirs, you can understand our legitimate and unavoidable impatience.

Source: Martin Luther King, Jr., Why We Can't Wait (New York: Harper & Row, 1963), p. 70.

Depending on the grade level, the teacher could make one of the following two assignments:

1. *Middle level:* Make a poster showing Martin Luther King Jr. and his use of direct action to end these economic, social, political, and cultural forms of segregation.

2. *Advanced middle school and high school level:* Write a five paragraph essay outlining Martin Luther King Jr.'s response to the Birmingham clergy using the ESP+C strategy.

With both assignments, consider having your students ponder what this document can tell us about the culture of the South with regard to race relations on the eve of the March on Washington (August 1963) and the passage of the Civil Rights Act of 1964. Also, note the Crossover that Dr. King makes in referencing the Constitution and the Declaration in his phrase "God-given rights." Consider making this exercise into an Intersection (see Chapter 4).

For Advanced Placement students consider using an essay question combining ESP+C with historiography.

AP Essay Question

In his struggle against second-class citizenship in the United States, the Reverend Dr. Martin Luther King Jr. once commented, "It may be true that the law cannot make a man love me, but it can stop him from lynching me, and I think that's pretty important."

In his book *Customs in Common: Studies in Traditional Popular Culture,* the historian E. P. Thompson (1991) concluded:

> Because law belongs to people, and is not alienated, or delegated, it is not thereby made necessarily more "nice" and tolerant, more cosy and folksy. It is only as nice and as tolerant as the prejudices and norms of the folk allow. For some of its victims the coming of a distanced (if alienated) Law and a bureaucratized police must have felt as a liberation of the tyranny of one's "own." (pp. 530–531)

Assess the validity of Thompson's statement with regard to the crime of lynching and the existence of Jim Crow justice, both legal and extralegal in the United States between 1930 and 1955.

The dates I used here anchor two important events. I selected these because they represent two types of justice, the trial of the Scottsboro Boys as an example of Jim Crow justice in the 1930s that before the young men were exonerated many people referred to as a "legal lynching," and the extralegal lynching of Emmett Till in Money, Mississippi, in 1955. Other dates would certainly be valid; in fact one could begin with the Till case and extend to the murders of the three Civil Rights workers, Michael Schwerner, James Chaney, and Andrew Goodman, in July of 1964. One could even extend this beyond African Americans to immigrants and begin with the lynching of Leo Frank in Georgia in 1915 and ending with the executions of Nicola Sacco and Bartolomeo Vanzetti in Massachusetts in 1927.

In his insightful book *Divided We Stand*, Jim Percoco (2001) suggests the use of music and lyric analysis as another means of stimulating student interest. For an added dimension to this unit, consider playing Vicki Lawrence or Reba McEntire's version of the song "The Night the Lights Went Out in Georgia" with its memorable refrain referring to the night "backwoods" Southern justice hung "an innocent man."

Consider having the students evaluate this expression of "lawless" culture along with Dr. King and E. P. Thompson. Conclude the unit by asking students to consider whether the lawlessness in this period was purely a "southern" phenomenon as the lyrics to the song suggest or rooted in larger economic, social, political, and cultural traditions in the nation as a whole.

Recognizing Washington's Contributions

One application of the ESP+C method is as a mental organizer and writing strategy. It is intended mainly for middle school students, again as training wheels for writing exercises like the five paragraph essay using historical content. In the spirit of the early content that most middle school standards cover, we will take the basic question, who was George Washington? When students encounter a question like this on an assessment, they have a number of decisions to make. Would it be sufficient to identify Washington simply as the first president of the United States, a general in the American Revolution, or even as a gentleman farmer? While all of these are technically correct, most history and studies teachers would argue that they offer little information. The central question remains, what is the overall significance of Washington to American history? For social studies teachers in particular, what is his impact on the nation?

Take the response to the same question using the basic ESP+C model. First the students would have to decide what, of the things they could recall about Washington, was his most significant contribution to the nation. In this case his role as the first president of the new Republic is the broadest and could be adapted to encompass the other things they were able to brainstorm. They would then apply ESP+C.

George Washington was the first president of the United States and as such made an important contribution to the social, economic, and political growth of the new nation. If the students were able to remember the other two items, gentleman farmer and general, they could flesh out the response even more, using the same formula by simply plugging in and explaining these items in the appropriate categories.

A Response Using ESP+C

George Washington was the first president of the United States and as such made an important contribution to the social, economic, and political growth of the new nation. Socially Washington set much of the etiquette related to the presidency. Rejecting the idea that the president should behave like a king, he brought dignity to the office without excessive pomp. Politically Washington helped to set many of the traditions associated with the presidency. From his decision to limit his time in office to two terms to his appointment of the first cabinet, Washington's influence continues to be felt in key aspects of American politics. In terms of economics, Washington's appointment of Alexander Hamilton as his secretary of the Treasury had a major impact on the new nation. Washington's faith in Hamilton's ability to set a sound monetary policy ultimately helped to put the new nation on more stable footing and insured that the revolution that the colonists had bravely fought to win their independence from England would be preserved. Today Washington remains a cultural icon. Many streets, towns, and even structures are named for him, and his image is on the one-dollar bill.

Teachers can help prompt students to make these decisions by modeling ESP+C in the classroom and consistently revisiting it during homework reviews and class discussion.

Understanding Historical Terms

One of the benefits of the ESP+C model is that it not only helps students to think critically about history but also helps them to develop a greater degree of what E. D. Hirsh called cultural literacy (Hirsch, 1987). Therefore when they encounter a historical term used out of context, they at least have a fighting chance of figuring out the context even if they have never encountered the term before.

Take, for example, an article by Ehsan Ahrari (2006) in *Asia Times Online,* which concluded, "Even by assigning the best possible intention to the decision of George W. Bush to invade Iraq, the fact of the matter is that Iraq will become his Waterloo." Even a student with passing familiarity with the term *Waterloo,* Napoleon's ill fated last battle after returning from exile, might be at a loss for its connection to an American war more than 180 years later. The reader would not only have to be able to identify Waterloo but explain its economic, social, political, and cultural significance to understand its application to another not quite congruous scenario in the present day. By using the ESP+C strategy, teachers can encourage students to look for these connections when they are looking up or encountering a term for the first time, be it in their primary textbook or in the newspaper. In this way they will always be probing not only the immediate meaning or context of historical terms, but also their deeper meaning, since knowing the ESP+C of a person or event begs the larger question of why this is important and demands that students address this in at least four ways, its economic, social, political, and cultural significance.

Correlating With the National Social Studies Standards

A teacher using the national social studies standards could easily construct a unit using the ESP+C strategy incorporating both content and skills.

For instance, in Figure 6.1, look at the indicator concerning immigration under Standard 2A. Grade level 7–12 asks students to "distinguish between the 'old' and 'new' immigration in terms of its volume and the immigrants' ethnicity, religion, language, place of origin, and motives for emigrating from their homelands." This again is a perfect opportunity to have students apply ESP+C, especially since the indicator highlights their need to be able to identify multiple causes for a movement or event. The process of distinguishing between the "old" and "new" immigration invites students to uncover the social, economic, political, and cultural causes that led people to leave their homelands for the United States. It also directs them to compare the experience of the new immigrants with those of the old. If one were to reflect on the example of the Irish, the Potato Famine that struck Ireland in the 1840s was significant in terms of its devastating economic impact on the Irish people but also the social, economic, and cultural problems it exacerbated between Ireland and England. This is the type of first-step historical thinking that a unit using ESP+C can yield.

The ESP+C strategy encourages students to think like social scientists employing multi-causality rather than allowing them to assign a single cause to a problem by picking from a preset list. Any military excursion is going to have social, economic, political, and cultural motivations, benefits, and consequences. We find these from the Thirty Years War to the Nazis' decision to invade Ethiopia to the War on Terror. Having students reflect critically about these using the ESP+C strategy encourages them to dig, sort, and quantify their answers. More important, however, the strategy provides students with a tool to not only identify but also understand historical content in a way that helps them take the first steps toward developing critical thinking and reading comprehension skills that will contribute to their overall intellectual growth and development.

Using ESP+C With the KWL Strategy

The ESP+C strategy can also be used with a variety of other teaching techniques and strategies, several of which I have already mentioned. Many middle school teachers say that they like to use ESP+C in conjunction with a KWL chart. KWL is a reading instructional strategy that begins with the students engaging in a brainstorming session to determine everything they know about a topic (Ogle, 1986). That information is recorded in the K column of a KWL chart. Students then create a list of questions about what they want to know about the subject. These questions are listed in the W column of the chart. Either during or at the conclusion of the reading, students record their answers to these questions. The new information they uncover is then placed in the L or "learned" column of the KWL.

In history and social studies the ESP+C-enhanced KWL allows students to better organize and focus their questions by encouraging them to look for those items that are most often associated with historical significance. They would begin the same as in the standard KWL by recording what

FIGURE 6.1   National Standards for History Era 6—The Development of the Industrial United States (1870–1900)

STANDARD 2

Massive immigration after 1870 and how new social patterns, conflicts, and ideas of national unity developed amid growing cultural diversity.

Standard 2A

The student understands the sources and experiences of the new immigrants.

Grade Level	Therefore, the student is able to
7–12	Distinguish between the "old" and "new" immigration in terms of its volume and the immigrants' ethnicity, religion, language, place of origin, and motives for emigrating from their homelands. [Analyze multiple causation]
5–12	Trace patterns of immigrant settlement in different regions of the country and how new immigrants helped produce a composite American culture that transcended group boundaries. [Reconstruct patterns of historical succession and duration]
5–12	Assess the challenges, opportunities, and contributions of different immigrant groups. [Examine historical perspectives]
7–12	Evaluate how Catholic and Jewish immigrants responded to religious discrimination. [Obtain historical data]
9–12	Evaluate the role of public and parochial schools in integrating immigrants into the American mainstream. [Analyze cause-and-effect relationships]

Standard 2B

The student understands "scientific racism," race relations, and the struggle for equal rights.

Grade Level	Therefore, the student is able to
7–12	Analyze the scientific theories of race and their application to society and politics. [Examine the influence of ideas]
5–12	Explain the rising racial conflict in different regions, including the anti-Chinese movement in the West and the rise of lynching in the South. [Explain historical continuity and change]
9–12	Analyze the role of new laws and the federal judiciary in instituting racial inequality and in disfranchising various racial groups. [Evaluate the implementation of a decision]
9–12	Analyze the arguments and methods by which various minority groups sought to acquire equal rights and opportunities guaranteed in the nation's charter documents. [Identify issues and problems in the past]

FIGURE 6.2   Thomas Jefferson

K What I KNOW	W What I WANT to Know (ESP+C)	L What I LEARNED (ESP+C)
Jefferson was from Virginia Jefferson wrote the Declaration of Independence Jefferson owned slaves Jefferson was the 3rd President of the United States	What was the economic, social, political, and cultural significance of the things that Jefferson did? How did they impact him personally and how did they impact the nation? How do they impact us even to this day?	Jefferson's efforts and actions as one of the founding fathers and as the third president of the United States had a definite social, economic, and political impact on the new Republic. For example, Jefferson's purchase of Louisiana doubled the size of the United States . . .

they already knew. Then they would ask questions rooted in ESP+C about what else they would like to know. In the final column they would be asked to write a paragraph summarizing the economic, social, political, and cultural significance of the person or event they were asked to study. Figure 6.2 shows a KWL on Thomas Jefferson using ESP+C.

How could you use the ESP+C strategy and a KWL chart to have your students examine the political cartoon in Figure 6.3? Which of your state standards or the National History standards would you use here? This example is correlated to Louisiana's social studies standards:

LA Standard 34. Identify the characteristics of the 1920s and describe the cultural changes that resulted (e.g., Harlem Renaissance, prohibition, women's suffrage) (H-1B- H11)

2. Investigate the long-term effects of reform movements, such as women's suffrage and prohibition (e.g., the 18th, 19th, and 21st Amendments to the Constitution) (Louisiana Department of Education, 2004)

Ask students to assess the ESP+C of the image with regard to social, economic, political, and cultural changes for women in the 1920s. Be sure to have your students consider if these changes affected all women or just women in certain segments of American society.

QUESTIONS FOR REVIEW AND REFLECTION

1. State content standards are literally full of references to economic, social, political, and cultural (ESP+C) causes of events and the like. Review your state content standards for any such references. Make notations to

FIGURE 6.3

"TWO'S COMPANY, THREE'S A CROWD.
——Chapin in the St. Louis *Republic.*

Source: From the *Literary Digest,* June 28, 1919. Originally from the *St. Louis Republic (Chapin).* San Francisco Academy of Comic Art Collection, The Ohio State University Cartoon Research Library.

specific standards that contain this language. How might you use the ESP+C method to teach this content and get students thinking about these broad categories of analysis?

2. The concept of remote viewing can produce exciting opportunities to explore history. Moving away from written assignments, consider having your students practice remote viewing by creating a picture or poster that illustrates the ESP+C of a historical event. How might you use primary sources and discussion to stimulate your students in preparation for such an exercise? Take a few moments to consider a few episodes or events in history that might lend themselves to such an exercise.

REFERENCES

Ahrari, E. (2006). Bush and Barney's path to Waterloo. *Asia Times Online,* October 3. Retrieved March 20, 2008, from http://www.atimes.com/atimes/Front_Page/HJ03Aa01.html

Bradley Commission on History in Schools. (1989). Building a history curriculum: Guidelines for teaching history in schools. *The History Teacher, 23,* 7–35.

Drake, F & Nelson, L. (2004). *Engagement in teaching history.* Upper Saddle River, NJ: Pearson.

Hirsch, E. D. Jr.. (1987). *Cultural literacy.* Boston, MA: Houghton Mifflin Company.

King Jr., Martin Luther. (1963). *Why we can't wait.* New York: Harper & Row.

Louisiana Department of Education. (2004). *Division of Student Standards & Assessments Grade-Level Expectations–Social Studies.* Retrieved March 20, 2008, from http://www .doe.state.la.us/Lde/saa/1843.html

Ogle, D. (1986). K-W-L: A teaching model that develops active reading of expository text. *The Reading Teacher, 39,* 564–570.

Percoco, J. A. (2001). *Divided we stand: Teaching about conflict in U.S. History.* Portsmouth, NH: Heinemann.

Stauffer, R. (1975). *Directing the reading/thinking process.* New York: Harper & Row.

Thompson, E. . (1991). *Customs in common: Studies in traditional popular culture.* New York: The New Press.

RESOURCES AND FURTHER READING

Beyer, B. K. (1980). Using writing to learn in history. *The History Teacher 13,* 167–178.

This is a good source for those looking for ways link writing instruction with historical content. Beyer demonstrates ways that teachers can use writing not solely as a method of emulation but as an integral part of the process of teaching and learning history.

Davey, B. (1983). Think-aloud—modeling the cognitive processes of reading comprehension. *Journal of Reading, 27,* 44–47.

This is a very useful article on the Think Aloud approach to reading that would work well with ESP+C in its active engagement of students' prior knowledge and its emphasis on having students revisit their predictions through the course of analyzing a reading passage.

Kneeshaw, S. (1992). KISSing in the history classroom: Simple writing activities that work. *Social Studies, 83(4),* 176–179.

This is a good article chock full of ways to incorporate short writing assignments into history instruction. Many of these would work well with ESP+C and other methods in this book as well.

Lasear, D. (1991). *Seven ways of teaching: The artistry of teaching with multiple intelligences.* Palatine, IL: Skylight.

This is a great book with many neat ideas about addressing multiple intelligences in the classroom. Many of the methods in this book would work well with ESP+C for history and social studies teachers.

Ogle, D. M. (2000). Make it visual: A picture is worth a thousand words. In M. McLaughlin & M. E. Vogt (Eds.). *Creativity and innovation in content area teaching* (pp. 55–71). Norwood, MA: Christopher-Gordon.

This is good resource on how to incorporate visuals including art into your teaching.

Palincsar, A. S., & Brown, A. L. (1986). Interactive teaching to promote independent learning from text. *The Reading Teacher, 39,* 771–777.

This is another really good article emphasizing reading comprehension skills through reciprocal teaching in small groups that could easily be applied to history and social studies content areas. Using ESP+C in conjunction with this method would add a beneficial layer of content specific analysis for history and social studies teachers.

Sippola, A. E. (1995). K-W-L-W. *The Reading Teacher, 48,* 542–543.

This is a very good article on using the K-W-L that suggests a modification to the chart for "What I want to know" as a means of encouraging student interest and research.

Seixas, P. (1994). Students' understanding of historical significance. *Theory and research in social education, 23,* 281–304.

In this thought provoking essay based on a limited study of Canadian tenth graders, Seixas reflects on how careful consideration of what students recognize as historically significant could greatly enhance our understanding about the teaching and the learning of history.

Young, K. M. & Leinhardt, G. (1998). Writing from primary documents: A way of knowing history. *Written Communication, 15(1),* 25–68.

This is a useful study by two professors that examines ways teachers might improve student writing as well as content knowledge through exercises like document-based questions that encourage document analysis and interpretation, source synthesis, and writing.

Conclusion

The value of an idea lies in the using of it.

—Thomas Alva Edison

In my observations as a teacher, former director of social studies education, and lifetime learner, I have grown to admire those teachers who are able to transform the most abstract concepts into tangible lessons for students. This involves a great deal of creativity, often demonstrated in a teacher's ability to find novel ways to communicate old truths. Teaching is very personal. Every teacher has his or her own style. It is also a creative exercise. The very nature of the act makes it so.

Margaret Boden, research professor of Cognitive Science at the University of Sussex in England, defines two types of creativity that she calls improbabilist and impossibilist. Improbabilist creativity, she observes, involves making new connections between facts and ideas within existing conceptual frames. Impossibilist creativity, on the other hand, goes much deeper and involves the transformation of the conceptual frameworks themselves in ways that allow the once unthinkable to become possible (Boden, 1994, pp. 519–520). This type of creativity is most often associated with the world-changing discoveries of great thinkers like Albert Einstein or Bill Gates who literally transformed the world with the force of their ideas.

While it is impossible to compare, Boden cautions us not to discount the power of improbabilist creativity and the impact it can have on the individual mind. Although the ideas may not be new or even very potent, there is definite power when a teacher is able to open up individuals to the process of learning and self-discovery that is education. While this may not change the world, it can open a whole new universe in the minds of individuals setting them on a path of inquiry that knows no bounds.

The methodologies presented in this book proceed from Boden's improbabilist definition of creativity. Perhaps there was little here that surprised you in the sense of being completely new. In fact, a good deal of my work represents the recasting of familiar ideas and thus would not have been possible without the yeoman work of others in the field. My hope is that what is here has stimulated your creativity and perhaps given you a fresh perspective and a few novel methods of getting students excited about history and of opening up new avenues of inquiry for them as well.

I have privileged a model of history education built on methods and activities that are heavily experiential. As my grandmother often reminded me, as I was busy studying to complete my undergraduate degrees in the early 1990s, some of the best teachers have never set foot in a classroom. "Don't forget," she would chide me on those rare occasions when I made it home for a few days, "there is more to life than books you always got your head stuck in." "You won't be able to share any of those things you are studying," she advised, usually over a piece of her legendary peach cobbler, "if you haven't lived and experienced nothing in this world." I am not sure I really took her words to heart until I was actually in the classroom looking for ways to make what I had to teach interesting and relevant to my students. The most creative history teachers for me bridge the gap between the world of academics and the practical experience my grandmother counseled. Like most scholars, such teachers feed an insatiable appetite for knowledge, constantly digesting new information. However, they present this knowledge in a hybrid approach in the classroom, making the information accessible by transmitting that knowledge through learned experience and having students do rather than take notes about history. They transform the past from something that happened yesterday into something that continues to affect us in the present. They reveal the past with the proper balance of preparation and inspiration by allowing students to discover it influencing every aspect of our lives. Last, they reveal themselves as fellow learners in a way that de-centers without distorting the teacher–student relationship. They model scholarship not by simply talking about it but by doing it, showing their own engagement with history through the creative means by which they convey the subject.

This is the main idea behind Haunted History and CSI: to get students to not only inquire about but research and discuss the world around them—in short, to involve them in the process of discovery that is historical research. Ideally this will encourage them to recognize the importance of history to their own lives. More concretely it will hone their critical thinking and problem solving skills as they apply them in addressing historical mysteries and crime scenes designed to help them become better acquainted with our collective history, their own communities, and the wider world.

In moving beyond the textbook and making the community our classrooms, we can also demonstrate the concept of agency and the

Intersection. As we help our students to understand the interplay of action and reaction, choice and chance, that underlies the historical process, we can further open them up to their own role in a participatory democracy. Helping them become co-agents of their own learning is the first step toward the ultimate goal of helping them to become engaged and responsible citizens who recognize the importance of being conscientious and productive members of society. Using methods like the mock legal contests or even introducing students to the ongoing interpretation of our Constitution through a character like SCOTUS is part of the equation. Using such methods not only acquaints students with the functions of government, but illustrates how individuals and groups have influenced that process and how the students can do the same using the most potent lessons from history.

This requires clear thinking as well as the ability to make connections about issues in the present with strong ties to the past. ESP+C and Historical Fingerprinting demonstrate ways to help students do what is not necessarily natural, namely appreciate the continuing influence of the past on the present and the running dialogue about the nature of our politics, economy, society, and culture. Engaging students using primary sources and exposing them to the idea of history as an ongoing conversation and debate about the meaning of the past is certainly not new. The ideas and methods presented here try to present fresh ways to approach these well-established methods of instruction. I hope that they have stimulated and inspired your own sense of creativity in crafting lessons that will challenge both you and your students.

REFERENCE

Boden, M. A. (1994). Précis of the creative mind: Myths and mechanisms. *Behavioural and Brain Sciences, 17*, 519–570.

RESOURCES AND FURTHER READING

Boden, M. A. (1990). *The creative mind: Myths and mechanisms.* London: Weidenfeld & Nicholson.

Boden, M. A. (Ed.). (1996). *Dimensions of creativity.* Cambridge, MA: MIT Press.

Lawson, B. (1997). *How designers think: The design process demystified.* Burlington, MA: Architectural Press.

Mithen, S. J. (1998). Creativity in human evolution and prehistory. New York: Routledge.

Index

CORWIN PRESS

The Corwin Press logo—a raven striding across an open book—represents the union of courage and learning. Corwin Press is committed to improving education for all learners by publishing books and other professional development resources for those serving the field of PreK–12 education. By providing practical, hands-on materials, Corwin Press continues to carry out the promise of its motto: **"Helping Educators Do Their Work Better."**

THE **American Institute** FOR HISTORY EDUCATION

"Well done is better than well said"

The American Institute for History Education is pleased to work with Corwin Press to publish *Teaching U.S. History Beyond the Textbook* by Dr. Yohuru Williams, our Vice President for History Education. AIHE was founded to provide history teachers with high quality professional development programs, firmly anchored in rich historical content, along with substantive historical lessons, activities, and resources to use in their classrooms. Dr. Williams has worked assiduously with AIHE over the past four years to provide these resources along with rich historical content to teachers participating in its TAH Grant programs in over 60 school districts throughout the country. This book will provide educators with engaging strategies and techniques to bring history to life in their classrooms.

CPSIA information can be obtained
at www.ICGtesting.com
Printed in the USA
FSHW012305240319
56636FS